BLESSED IN THE MESS

BLESSED
IN THE
MESS

How to Experience God's Goodness
in the Midst of Life's Pain

JOYCE MEYER

NEW YORK · NASHVILLE

FaithWords
Hachette Book Group
1290 Avenue of the Americas, New York, NY 10104
faithwords.com
twitter.com/faithwords

First Edition: September 2023

FaithWords is a division of Hachette Book Group, Inc. The FaithWords name and logo are trademarks of Hachette Book Group, Inc.

The publisher is not responsible for websites (or their content) that are not owned by the publisher.

The Hachette Speakers Bureau provides a wide range of authors for speaking events. To find out more, go to hachettespeakersbureau.com or email HachetteSpeakers@hbgusa.com.

FaithWords books may be purchased in bulk for business, educational, or promotional use. For information, please contact your local bookseller or the Hachette Book Group Special Markets Department at special.markets@hbgusa.com.

Library of Congress Cataloging-in-Publication Data has been applied for.

ISBNs: 978-1-5460-3734-7 (hardcover), 978-1-5460-0487-5 (large print), 978-1-5460-0035-8 (ebook)

Printed in the United States of America

LSC-C

Printing 1, 2023

CONTENTS

Life is often messy. We hear people say, "My life is a mess," or "This situation is a mess." What they mean is that life has become difficult, painful, or confusing. God never promises us a trouble-free existence. In fact, His Word teaches us to expect the opposite. Jesus says, "In the world you will have tribulation; but be of good cheer, I have overcome the world" (John 16:33 NKJV). In addition, the Bible is filled with instructions on how to handle ourselves when difficulty comes our way. Remaining patient, continuing to trust God when we don't understand what is going on, and staying positive are just three ways we are to respond when we feel life is a mess (Romans 12:12; Proverbs 3:5), and they are all for our benefit. No matter what unpleasant circumstances we may face, if we remain patient, trust God, and stay positive, we can enjoy life while He works on our problems.

Thankfully, trouble is not continuous in our lives. We also go through seasons that are peaceful and pleasant. But life does not *always* go as we would like, and we need to be prepared and strong spiritually for the times when it gets messy. It is important that we learn not to behave one way when we like our circumstances and another when we find them challenging. We need to be stable in every situation, and our ability to do so is based on our thinking and believing. If we think positively, expecting something good to come from our trouble, and if we trust God and remind ourselves that He is good, we can make it through difficulties more easily than if we are negative and don't trust Him.

Jesus has given us His peace, but He also tells us not to let ourselves be fearful, intimidated, worried, and unsettled (John 14:27

*You can be blessed in the
midst of trouble and pain.*

AMPC). The fact that God has given us
something doesn't mean we make good
use of it. Peace is available, but Jesus
says, "Do not *let* your hearts be troubled" (John 14:1, emphasis mine).

The message of this book is simple: We will all face trouble and
pain in life, but if we handle it the way God wants us to, we can be
blessed in the midst of it. In the Old Testament, Job endured great
trouble, but in the end, he was given twice as much as he had lost
(Job 42:10). This principle appears throughout God's Word. The
question is, do we want our troubles to make us better or worse?
Do we want our pain to make us pitiful or to make us powerful?
Since we will encounter trouble either way, why not let our difficulties make us better and stronger? Why not live in such a way
that we will end up better off than we were before the trouble
began? We should never waste our pain. We can learn something
from it, use it to stay out of trouble in the future, and let it inspire
and equip us to help other people.

There is a way to be blessed in the midst of your mess and to
receive God's reward at the end of it. In this book, I hope to show
you how to do it. We all have trouble, but not all of us handle it
well. If we don't, we can change, and thank God, we can always
change in positive ways. If you have not handled your problems
and pain well in the past, then with God's help, you can begin to
handle them better, starting now.

I have been in a serious relationship with God for more than
forty-five years. Like everyone, I began as a baby Christian, behaving like a baby and reacting emotionally every time life became
difficult or situations didn't go my way. However, over the years,
I have learned how to behave, and God's Word and His Spirit

have changed me. I can testify that the things that once upset me greatly do not disturb me at all now. Why? Because I know how they will end if I do what God asks me to do.

I am far from perfect. Just a few days ago, a situation threatened to ruin my plans for the day, and I became impatient and frustrated. My family started preaching my sermons back to me, which only added to my frustration. The good news is that within ten minutes, I felt peaceful and the day turned out as I had planned after all. There are times I don't behave properly, and I am still growing. But thankfully I have improved a lot, and I am determined not to let the devil steal the joy of my progress by causing me to focus on my remaining weaknesses. I know I will be strengthened in all my troubles as time goes by. God doesn't change us all at once; He does it little by little. Start thanking God for the little you have, and you will be given more.

> God changes you little by little.

I believe that learning to be stable in problematic situations is one of life's most important lessons. Unless we become stable, we will always be subject to upset and distress when our circumstances are unpleasant or painful, as they will be at times. Learn how to be blessed in your mess and come out better than you were when your difficulty began. Learn to use troubles to your advantage instead of letting the devil use them to weaken and perhaps defeat you. God has taught me how to do this, and I know He can teach you too.

PART 1

God Can Bless Your Mess

CHAPTER 1

The Double Blessing

Blessed are they who see beautiful things in humble places where other people see nothing.

Camille Pissarro[1]

I want to begin this book by telling you a story. It is my story, but it could be your story or the story of someone you know. We all have a story, and even if yours is different from mine, it is important to you and to God, and you can help someone else by telling it at the right time.

As a child, I was sexually abused by my father on a regular basis. This went on for many, many years. It was a horrible experience, to say the least. I'll spare you the terrible details, but it was a nightmare I would not want to live through again.

The house in which I grew up was filled with fear. I cannot remember ever being without fear during my childhood years. My father was controlling and just plain mean. He was physically abusive to my mother, and he basically ignored my brother except to curse at him when he was angry.

My mother knew my father abused me sexually, but she too lived and breathed fear. When I was in my fifties, she told me she was sorry for what she let my father do to me and went on to say, "I just couldn't face the scandal." In those days, incest was unheard of. It happened regularly, but no one talked about it—ever. I recall my father continually warning me never to tell anyone, which made no sense to me because he also said that what he was doing was good and that he did it because he loved me.

I reached out to some relatives to help me, but they didn't want to get involved. So, I eventually decided that, since no one would help me, I would survive and then leave home as soon as I finished high school. But before I share more of my story, I want to mention a life-changing experience that happened when I was quite young.

God Comes on the Scene

When I was nine years old, we were visiting my aunt and uncle, and I wanted to go to church with them. I also wanted to be saved. I don't know how I even knew what "being saved" meant, because I had received no spiritual training at home. But somehow, I knew I was a sinner and needed salvation. While my father was out getting drunk one Saturday night, I went to church with my aunt and uncle and walked to the altar at the close of the service. The pastor prayed with me, and I experienced an unmistakable cleansing of my soul. I knew that God had touched me. I was born again!

However, after that night, I received no subsequent teaching or training to help me grow spiritually. For that reason, as soon as I did something wrong, I thought I had lost my salvation. I remained in that condition for many years. I prayed hard for God to get me out of the situation I was in, but He didn't. He did, however, get me through it, and although my soul was damaged and needed healing as a result, I was also strong and determined to survive and thrive in life. I believe my determination was a gift from God.

We don't always understand why God doesn't deliver us from hard situations, but He always has a reason for His decisions, even when we can't see it. In my case, I believe He chose not to remove the difficulties so I could gain the experience I would need to do what I am doing now. I truly understand what people mean when they say they are hurting, and I am able to

> God always has a reason for His decisions, even when we can't see it.

have compassion for them because of the pain I have suffered. I also know that God will heal their wounded souls and broken hearts because He has healed mine.

The Bible says that Jesus gained obedience through the things He suffered, and this equipped Him to become the Author and

Source of our salvation (Hebrews 5:8–9 AMPC). I believe the same process often happens in the lives of those whom God intends to use to help others. As G. V. Wigram wrote, "Sorrows and trials are . . . like the sand and grit that polish a stone."[2]

To say I was a mess when I left home at the age of eighteen is an understatement. To the natural eye, I appeared to be fine. I was reasonably intelligent and could hold a good job. But I was terrible at relationships. I didn't know how to think properly, feel appropriately, or do what was right. I felt guilty about what had been done to me, and I was rooted in shame. I didn't like my personality, my looks, or anything else about myself. I operated in protection mode constantly and trusted no one, especially men. I had promised myself that once I got away from home, I would never allow myself to need anyone. I had a few casual friendships, but I kept those relationships at a safe distance and never allowed anyone to get very close to me.

Deciding not to need other people doesn't work, because God has created us to function together as a unit, not individually as loners. Not one of us has everything that is needed to live a good life by ourselves. We need other people who have gifts, abilities, and talents we do not have. People were not created to be alone.

If you have relationships that are a mess, let me assure you that God can change them and turn them into a blessing. Here is a story by a woman named Hannah that proves my point.

God Changes People's Hearts

I've always been a bit overprotective. So, when my brother's new girlfriend made a horrible first (and second, and third) impression, I jumped to the conclusion that he was settling for less than God's best for him.

When he was unwilling to listen to my critical observation, I decided to take matters into my own hands. I spouted off a few fiery words I'd never be able to take back in an attempt to push her far, far away. But she didn't run. In fact, she stood by his side stronger than ever. It was in that moment that I realized maybe I'd misjudged her.

I was embarrassed by my actions and began seeking God's mercy and forgiveness. And while I thought it was best if they broke up, I realized I never want my will to be done, but His. I began to pray that His plans would ultimately prevail. If my brother and his girlfriend were meant to be a couple, I asked God to change my heart.

And change my heart, He did. It wasn't noticeable at first, but little by little, the tainted lens through which I viewed her got a little less blurry. And she was no longer my enemy. In fact, I even began to see her beautiful heart.

Her love for Jesus became more and more apparent over time, and because of that, I was able to see that she actually loves my brother so beautifully. She's since forgiven me and I'm now gaining a sister-in-law, who is also my sister in Christ. What more could I ask for?

While I initially created quite a mess, God helped me realize I am so very blessed. He changed my heart and allowed me to see her through His eyes instead of my own.

If you're going through a sticky situation, I invite you to pray and ask God to lead the way. You never know; He may change your heart as well.

Jumping to conclusions about people before giving yourself time to truly get to know them is a mistake. Give people a chance before deciding to eliminate them from your life. Sometimes you will find they are worth including, as Hannah did. And sometimes you will find, as I did in the story below, that you need to end your relationship with them in order to enjoy the blessed life God wants you to live.

A Bad Relationship That Never Improved

When I was eighteen years old, I met a boy on a blind date. He had as many problems as I did—or more. After a short time of dating, we married, and I had another five years of misery and a ridiculous lifestyle. He frequently disappeared for months at a time, eventually returning and telling me how sorry he was. I always took him back. Neither of us knew what love was. He was a con man and petty thief who ended up in prison.

I married him because I was desperate, thinking no one would ever want me since I had been sexually abused. Desperate people do not make good decisions. I knew deep in my heart that the marriage probably would not work out, but I did it anyway. If I could go back and do it over again, would I marry him? Probably not, but I cannot say I regret it, because God brought a blessing out of the mess I had made.

> *Desperate people do not make good decisions.*

During the five years we were married, we were apart more than we were together, but I had one miscarriage and gave birth to one son during that time. While I was pregnant with my son, my husband left me, went to live with another woman, and told everyone the baby wasn't his. I was alone, living on the third floor of an apartment building during an extremely hot summer. I don't even think I had a fan, let alone air-conditioning. I was so miserable during that time that instead of gaining weight while pregnant, I lost thirty-five pounds. It was one of the darkest times in my life. However, God promises to give us treasures from the dark places, and He did give me my son.

> I will give you the treasures of darkness and hidden riches
> of secret places, that you may know that I, the Lord, who
> call you by your name, am the God of Israel.
>
> Isaiah 45:3 NKJV

While I was pregnant, when I could no longer work, my hairdresser and her mother let me live with them until the baby was born. Although I didn't live on the street, I was homeless in a way and totally dependent on people who were little more than strangers to help me.

When my son was born, my husband did show up at the hospital. The baby boy looked just like him, so there was no denying that the child was his. We left the hospital and literally had no place to live, so my husband called a Christian woman who had previously been married to one of his brothers, and she took us in.

Eventually, my son David grew up and became CEO of our world missions program, called Hand of Hope, at Joyce Meyer Ministries. He has personally helped to start feeding centers, hospitals, and medical mission programs. He has provided help for victims of sex trafficking, for building churches, and for the digging of water wells in more than forty countries in villages that have no clean water. As part of these programs, we always share the gospel. In addition, we are on television throughout the world in more than one hundred languages, and David has helped with this. When I was pregnant with him, I was in a very dark season in my life, but he has turned out to be a treasure that came out of that dark time.

During the time David and I lived with my husband's ex-sister-in-law, my husband left. As soon as I could, I got a job, an apartment, and a babysitter for David, and I tried to start life again. My husband came back once but soon left yet again. After that, I couldn't take it anymore and filed for divorce.

Out of desperation, I moved back home with my parents because I had no other option. I knew I would spend most of my time trying to avoid my father's sexual advances, but God had mercy on me. Soon after I moved into my parents' home, Dave Meyer pulled up in front of the house. He was there to pick up a young man he worked with who lived in the upstairs apartment.

In October 1966, I was outside washing my mother's car, and Dave started flirting with me. He asked me if I wanted to wash his car when I finished with mine. I replied, "Buddy, if you want your car washed, wash it yourself!" That was our beginning, but Dave still says he immediately knew I was the woman he wanted to marry. We married in January 1967, and thankfully, we are still married today. Even this is a miracle from God, because I was very difficult to get along with the first several years of our marriage. Today, we have four wonderful children, twelve grandchildren, and five great-grandchildren, and the number will continue to grow.

Blessed after a Mess

My first marriage was a mess that never changed. I had to get out of it, and God blessed me with a relationship with Dave. When we married, I had no idea what love was. I didn't know how to give it or receive it. Dave was a strong, committed Christian, and he asked me to go to church with him, which I was glad to do. I had loved God for as long as I could remember; I simply didn't know anything about the Bible or how to go about having relationship with God. I prayed when I was desperate, and my prayers consisted mostly of "God, help me." I struggled trying to be a Christian. I took confirmation classes and joined a church, hoping those experiences would change me, but they didn't. I learned basic Christian doctrine, but I did not learn how to live my daily life as a follower of Christ. Several years later, when Dave and I had three children, we moved to another area of town and went to another church for several years. We did make friends in that church and enjoyed going there, but once again, although I learned about God, I did not learn lessons to help me with my specific problems.

In 1976, I cried out to God to touch my life, and He did. I became hungry to study His Word. Shortly after that, I sensed Him calling me to teach the Bible and showing me that I would spread His Word, helping people around the world. Naturally speaking, this would have been impossible, but God chooses and uses the foolish things of the world—people who would be thrown away as trash—to confound the wise (1 Corinthians 1:26–31).

In those days, many people considered it unacceptable for women to teach the Bible, but I wasn't aware of that, so I started a Bible study at my workplace. I look back and wonder how I had the courage to do it because I had no idea what I was doing. But when God calls us, He also gives us a gift of faith to do what He asks us to do. I stepped out and He met me. As He taught me, I shared with others what He was teaching me.

I taught that Bible study for five years, eventually moving it into my home. Every Tuesday evening, twenty-five or thirty people would sit on the living room floor and sing a few songs, and I would teach God's Word. We would pray for one another, and it was wonderful. All the while, I was studying and learning. I took every opportunity I could find to study God's Word and read books that would help me understand the Bible. Dave and I also took a twelve-week Bible study course at our church that was designed to help develop leaders.

Those were wonderful years, yet they were some of the most painful of my life. I wanted to quit many times because it seemed that I had such a big dream, yet everything that was happening was so very small. But those experiences served a great purpose in my life. Saint Augustine said, "Trials come to prove and improve us,"[3] and this is so true.

> Lack gives us all an appreciation of abundance.

During those years, our family had financial needs. God made sure we had enough to survive, but we didn't have anything extra. This too was a test. We were giving more than ever, yet we seemed to have less than ever. But eventually, God began to bring increase to our finances. To this day, I am thankful for the lean years we experienced because I deeply appreciate everything God gives us now. I think lack gives us all an appreciation of abundance.

Eventually I got a job at a new local church in our city, and I worked there for five years. I became one of the associate pastors and had opportunities to do a lot of Bible teaching. Those were also years of testing because I was learning how to relate to authority and behave in a godly way when I didn't agree with those in authority over me. God taught me more than I can express during those years. Like the first five years of my teaching ministry, they were wonderful and extremely difficult at the same time. They were also vitally necessary, because I had to learn how to come under authority before I would be ready to be in authority.

> You must learn how to live under authority before you can be in authority.

I eventually did step out and start Joyce Meyer Ministries, and the ministry has grown gradually to what it is now. There have been many wonderful times and hard times, but they all have worked together for good (Romans 8:28).

The Promise That Changed My Life

While reading Isaiah 61:7 one day, I saw that God promises to give us a double portion to replace the shame from the past: "Instead of your shame you will receive a double portion, and instead of disgrace you will rejoice in your inheritance.

> God promises a double portion to replace shame from the past.

And so you will inherit a double portion in your land, and everlasting joy will be yours."

Many scriptures have been life-changing for me, and Isaiah 61:7 is certainly one of them. It gave me hope, and hope is a vital quality to have. Without hope, the heart becomes sick (Proverbs 13:12).

When we have hope, we live with the expectation that God will do something good for us. Hope is a powerful motivator. Anyone can have hope if they want to. All you need to do is expect (believe) that something good may happen to you at any time. There were many years when I expected and waited for the next bad thing to happen in my life. I was actually afraid to believe for good things, because I didn't want to be disappointed. I have changed, by God's grace. Now I expect good things all the time, and I encourage you to do the same.

If you have trouble being hopeful, start by saying aloud several times a day "Something good is going to happen to me, because God is good." You will find that the more you speak this and meditate on it in your thinking, the more you will believe it. By doing this, you are renewing your mind (Romans 12:2).

In the Amplified Bible, Classic Edition translation of Isaiah 61:7, the phrase "double portion" is rendered "twofold recompense." We don't hear the word *recompense* often, but it simply means "reward." Once I realized what this verse is saying, I was filled with hope that somehow God would pay me back for all the misery I went through during my early years. He is a God of justice, which means that He makes wrong things right. I knew that what my father had done to me was wrong, but I came to believe that God would make it up to me.

When I looked for promises similar to Isaiah 61:7, I found Job 42:10: "After Job had prayed for his friends, the Lord restored his fortunes and gave him twice as much as he had before." It seems that nobody in the world ever had it as bad as poor ol' Job, who experienced calamity after calamity (Job 1:13–19; 2:7–9), but God gave him double for his former trouble. This happened after he prayed for his friends who had treated him badly. He needed them to comfort him, but instead they blamed him for his problems. We can see from this that anyone who wants the double blessing cannot have it with unforgiveness in their heart. I had to forgive my dad and mom, and you also will have to forgive anyone you have anything against if you want to be blessed.

Another passage that speaks of a double blessing is 2 Kings 2:1–12. There, we read that Elisha received a double portion of Elijah's anointing because he asked for it and was faithful to Elijah to the end of his life.

Proverbs 6:30–31 teaches us that there is even a sevenfold blessing. If someone steals from us, this passage teaches that when they are caught, they will have to pay back seven times more than they stole. This also comforts me, because people have taken things from me at times, and I always pray for them and claim the sevenfold return.

In the early days of our television ministry, our program aired once a week on a big station that was doing well. Suddenly one day, they took us off the air, offering no explanation except that they were making changes in their programming. I felt like my heart was breaking because that station reached more people than any other station we were on, and we were not on many at that time.

I was angry and hurt, but God told us to release the situation to Him, let Him handle it, and to forgive them. We did, and about a year later, they approached us and asked us to go on their station daily—exactly a sevenfold return.

I have turned to Isaiah 61:7 many times over the years when I have become discouraged. Each time, this verse and others similar to it encourage me to keep believing that God will do great things in my life.

I Am Amazed

I am amazed at what God has done for me. When I look at where I started and where I am now, it is almost too good to be true. I share this story so you will believe that the same kinds of things can happen to you. God's Word has been true in my life. I have favor, open doors of opportunity, and a television program that airs in more than one hundred languages in two-thirds of the world. I've written 146 books, tens of millions of which have been sold or given free of charge to people in need around the world. I get to help hurting people and make their lives better through teaching them the Word of God. My story, which was so painful for me to live through, now gives people hope, and I'm glad God took me through it instead of delivering me

> Something you now think is your worst enemy may one day be your best friend.

from it. You may also find that a situation you now think is your worst enemy will one day be your best friend.

My mess has become my message and my ministry, and this happens to many people if they let it. It happened to me, it happened to Sawyer, and it can happen to you. Here is Sawyer's story:

My Mess Became My Ministry

Sometimes, it takes a little time to see how God will work something out in our lives. For me, it took nearly two decades.

It all started for me at just four years old. I remember sitting in my dad's new apartment, doing my best to listen as he explained a new reality to me: He didn't want to live with us anymore, so instead I'd visit him every so often.

Things were all right at first, but over the years, they got worse and worse. One day, my dad told me he didn't believe in God anymore and that I shouldn't either. Another time, he told me my mother was crazy and shouldn't be raising me. He lied, made up stories, and told me I was selfish for not believing what he told me to believe. Sometimes he shouted.

Most of my childhood was filled with doubt—doubt about myself, my life, and my faith. As the verbal and emotional abuse got worse over time, I questioned why God would let me stay in that situation—month after month and year after year. I wanted to know what the plan was.

I remember the day I got my answer. It was my senior year of high school. As I left school to go home that day, I saw one of my classmates sitting at a table, crying. It turns out her father verbally abused her, shouting and screaming at her constantly and telling her she was worthless. Her parents were divorced, and because she wasn't yet eighteen, she still had to participate in visitation. She felt trapped.

That was the first time I was able to comfort someone with my story, to let them know they weren't alone, and to tell them that God could take something terrible and redeem it in a way that brings comfort and healing to someone else.

As the years have gone by, God has put me in the right places at the right times to help so many people in need with my story. I thank Him every day that when I nearly lost faith in Him, He never lost faith in me.

God has allowed Sawyer and me to help people facing situations like those we've gone through. As great as this is, more important is the relationship we have with God through Jesus.

I no longer feel guilty all the time. When I sin, I am able to quickly repent, receive forgiveness, and not feel burdened with guilt that Jesus has already taken care of through His sacrifice on the cross. I know for certain that God loves me unconditionally, and I truly believe that no matter what happens, He will work it out for my good.

I want you to be excited as you read this book. It is a book about going through trials and troubles, but it is also a book about how hard times can bring you closer to God than you could ever imagine and how you can be blessed right in the middle of your mess.

To experience blessing in the midst of your mess, you will need to make some decisions and take some actions that won't be easy. This includes keeping a good attitude during trouble; being thankful when there doesn't seem to be anything to be thankful for; forgiving people who don't deserve to be forgiven or who have abused, hurt, or abandoned you; being patient; staying positive; and making other choices you'll read about later in the book. The adjustments you may need to make will come in various forms and in many situations, but the double blessing will be worth them all.

Camille Pissarro's quote at the beginning of this chapter says, "Blessed are they who see beautiful things in humble places where other people see nothing." We are blessed when we can face our pain and our problems and know deep in our hearts that God will

> God offers us treasures in the darkness.

work something good out of them. Sad indeed are the people who have trouble and nothing but darkness and despair, but God offers us treasures in the darkness—hope, faith, and a double blessing. What an exciting way to live!

> Return to the stronghold [of security and prosperity], you prisoners of hope; even today do I declare that I will restore double your former prosperity to you.
>
> Zechariah 9:12 AMPC

CHAPTER 2

Who Made This Mess?

You cannot escape the responsibility of tomorrow by evading it today.

Abraham Lincoln[4]

Life can become a mess for all kinds of reasons and in many different ways. People often use the word *trouble* to describe their mess, their pain, or a particular stress in their life. They may say, "I'm having trouble at work," "I'm having trouble raising a teenager," "I'm having trouble moving forward after the divorce," "I'm having financial trouble," or "I'm having a little trouble with my blood pressure." The Bible does mention *trouble* specifically, along with various specific troubles we may face. Depending on which translation we read, it also refers to difficulties in other terms, including *trials*, *tests*, *temptation*, *hardship*, *tribulation*, *affliction*, *persecution*, and *suffering*.

All trouble tests us. It tests our character and determination to serve God. The apostle James writes that we should be joyful when we encounter trials (James 1:2). Why should we be joyful in the midst of trials and tests? James 1:3–4 says that they will work patience and perseverance in us, and when patience and perseverance have finished their work, we will be mature and complete, lacking in nothing we need in life.

> God uses our problems to test and mature us.

God doesn't cause our problems, but He does use them to test and mature us. I am sure most of us would admit that we have grown more spiritually during hard times than through easy ones. We grow during hard times because they force us to use our faith and press into God as never before. When we exercise our faith in God, it increases. We begin with little faith, but as we use it, our faith can grow to become great. The greater our faith is, the less tests and tribulations disturb us. We learn from God's Word and life's experiences (Proverbs 3:13 AMPC), and every time we go through something difficult and don't give up, we see that God is good and faithful and that we can trust Him. We also learn that we are stronger than we may have thought we were and that all problems eventually come to an end.

Maturity includes taking responsibility for the messes in our lives. When I say that we should take responsibility for our mess, I don't necessarily mean that the trouble you have is your fault. It could be, but it may not be. Satan attacks us, God tests us, and we live in a wicked world full of sin that causes difficulty of all kinds, some of which we cannot avoid. But no matter the source of our problem, we must take responsibility for facing it and going through it in a godly way. If we have sinned, we should admit it and repent, meaning we change our mind for the better and turn in another direction (the godly direction). When we sin and repent, God will not only forgive us, but He will also help us deal with the problem.

> *Maturity includes taking responsibility for the messes in our lives.*

People's natural inclination is to blame others for their troubles or their bad behavior. I did this for years, and it only kept me in the same place, doing the same thing over and over and getting nowhere. Jesus says, "The truth will set you free" (John 8:32). But for this to happen, we must receive the truth, apply it to ourselves, and stop making excuses and blaming others for our bad behavior.

Through many years of practice, I became an expert at avoiding and evading the truth about my behavior. Anytime I misbehaved, in my mind, it was always someone else's fault. Had they done something differently, I reasoned, I wouldn't have been upset and acted badly. It took me a long time to realize I was responsible for myself and my behavior and that no matter what anyone else did, God still expected me to behave in godly ways. The truth is, we grow spiritually when we obey God even when it isn't comfortable or convenient.

> We grow spiritually when we obey God even when it isn't comfortable or convenient.

Do you want to grow spiritually and become spiritually mature? If so, there is only one option, which is to obey God, whether obedience is easy or hard.

The fact that God asks us to make godly choices while others seem to do otherwise may seem unjust. But this is what Jesus did for us, and we are to follow in His footsteps. No matter what anyone else does, even when it is wrong, we are still responsible to do what is right. Each of us will stand before God and give an account of ourselves, not an account of someone else's choices.

Many people stumble in their walk with God when they feel they must act in a godly way while other people do not. They refuse to do their part unless the other party involved does theirs. "It isn't fair" becomes an excuse for not obeying God and not changing. God doesn't want excuses; He wants obedience. Waiting for someone else to make the first move in the right direction reveals spiritual immaturity. I believe the person who apologizes or says "I'm sorry" first is the one who is most spiritually mature. Romans 12:18 says, "If it is possible, as far as it depends on you, live at peace with everyone." Do everything possible to be at peace with people and work to keep all strife out of your life.

Learning that I didn't have to *want* to do the right thing in order to do it has helped me greatly. We can feel a situation is unfair and still make the choice that is right for us. We can feel that what God is asking of us is too hard but still obey Him. Our feelings matter and are a big part of our lives, but we cannot make our choices according to them because they are not reliable.

> *You can feel that what God is asking of you is too hard but still obey Him.*

Perhaps this has never occurred to you, but Jesus did not want to go to the cross and suffer as He did. While He was praying in the Garden of Gethsemane, He asked God, if possible, to take the cup of suffering from Him (Matthew 26:39). He also said to God, "Yet not as I will, but as you will." Then in verse 42, we read: "He went away a second time and prayed, 'My Father, if it is not possible for this cup to be taken away unless I drink it, may your will be done.'" He was basically saying, "I don't want to do this, but, Father, I want what You want more than I want what I want." We should have the same attitude when it comes to obeying God.

Blame Has Been Around a Long Time

Blaming others for our wrongdoings has been around since the beginning of time. Adam and Eve did it in the Garden of Eden. Satan tempted Eve, and when God confronted her, she blamed the serpent. Adam blamed Eve for his sin and even blamed God for giving her to him (Genesis 3:12–13). However, God punished Adam, Eve, and the serpent, so apparently, they all bore some responsibility. Unless

> *Unless you take responsibility for your actions, you will never be free from their consequences.*

we take responsibility for our actions, we will never be free from their consequences.

A situation similar to Adam and Eve's took place with Abram and Sarai (later named Abraham and Sarah). God had promised them a son (Genesis 15:1–4; 17:15–16, 19), but when they grew tired of waiting for the promise to come to pass, they took matters into their own hands. Sarai gave her handmaiden Hagar to her husband as a secondary wife so she could claim Hagar's child as her own. After Hagar became pregnant, she despised Sarai, and Sarai blamed Abram for the wrong she suffered (Genesis 16:1–5). This is amazing because Sarai is the one who came up with this plan and talked Abram into going along with it. Then, when it went wrong, she blamed him.

For years, I blamed my ungodly behavior on the fact that I had been sexually abused by my father. Although that abuse did cause anger, self-pity, selfishness, jealousy, insecurity, and other negative consequences, I could not keep using it as an excuse to continue to behave badly if I wanted to be free from my dysfunctional actions.

When Adam and Eve realized they had sinned, they hid from God (Genesis 3:8). Jonah didn't want to preach to the people of Nineveh, and he tried to hide from God (Jonah 1:1–3). But the result was that he was swallowed by a huge fish and stayed inside the fish for three days until he repented (Jonah 1:17; 2:1–9). Hiding or running from our problems never works to our benefit. It only increases our troubles until we humble ourselves and obey God.

> *Hiding from your problems never works to your benefit.*

Being responsible causes us to have to face or deal with a situation or to be accountable for something. Taking responsibility is hard. To say "This is my fault, and I take responsibility for it" is humbling, but it is also the first step toward freedom, even if you admit it only to yourself and God.

We rarely take responsibility for our messes. For example, if we are overweight, we say it is because our metabolism is slow or we have a chemical imbalance, even if we do not have a diagnosis.

Rarely do we simply admit that we eat too much and exercise too little. As we get older, our metabolism does slow down, and we have to adjust our eating. I read that every ten years our metabolism slows down and we lose some muscle mass, so we have to compensate for that by either eating less or exercising more.

Regarding weight, there are situations in which being overweight is the result of a medication, a genetic problem, a hormone imbalance, a thyroid issue, or some other cause. But often, it results from simply eating more than we should. When this is the case, admitting it to ourselves is the best thing we can do. It may be hard, but just because something is hard doesn't mean we can't do it.

I once read that only a fool thinks he can always do what he has always done, and I like this statement. It taught me a lot because I read it at a time when I needed to make some lifestyle changes and didn't want to admit to myself that I simply could not do what I had always done.

I cannot eat as much now as I did when I was twenty-five years old and maintain the same weight. I made excuses for a long time and then finally faced the truth. Now I eat a little less. I cannot work as hard as I once did unless I want to get sick. So now I work, but I also take time to rest and recover after periods of working hard.

Another example of not taking responsibility has to do with finances. People may blame their financial problems on their employer for not paying them enough money, or they may blame the world and high prices. Some people blame the devil and say he is attacking them when they struggle financially. But in reality, people may simply be spending beyond their means or not giving what they should give to God's work.

Before blaming anyone else for your problems, ask God to show you if you have opened a door for the problem. This is important not so you can feel guilty but so you can do what is needed to make the situation better.

Where Have All the Responsible People Gone?

One of the biggest problems in our world today is that so many people don't take responsibility for themselves. They want someone else to take care of them. This is one of the biggest mistakes a person can make. We cannot have respect for ourselves or from others unless we take responsibility for ourselves.

> You cannot have respect from others unless you take responsibility for yourself.

Being responsible was once part of being honorable and having good character, but most people don't value these qualities as people did years ago. Some people want to do as they please, avoid hard work and responsibility, and then have someone else clean up the messes they make along the way.

Many times, young adult children want to make their own decisions, and then, when they get in trouble because they have made bad decisions, they want their parents to fix the problems they created. We all want to help our children if they are in need, but rescuing them isn't always helping them.

We need to be responsible to get to work on time, do a good job while we are there, take care of our possessions, pay our bills on time, not spend more than we make, and dozens of other things. When we do what is right, we will enjoy our lives. When we don't, we will have messes of our own making. God is merciful, and we can recover from bad choices, but our first step toward recovery is to take responsibility for them. Then we should start consistently doing what is right. Every good decision we make will help us recover from a bad one made in the past.

Even our mistakes can be valuable if we will learn from them. In all things, God works for the good of those who love Him and are called according to His purpose (Romans 8:28). This is a wonderful promise, and it is one way we are assured that we can be blessed in our mess. I have seen God take my messes and turn them into messages that have helped a lot of people many times. He doesn't waste anything and will use even our mistakes for our good if we trust Him to do so.

I recently made an emotional decision instead of a wise one, and it caused a lot of work for me and some other people. Had I made a better choice, the extra work would have been avoided. When the situation didn't work out and I had to take responsibility for the fact that it didn't go well, I was tempted to feel guilty. But I have been around that mountain before in my life, and I know guilt doesn't do any good and it isn't God's will. I repented and apologized to the people affected negatively by my decision and then counted it as a good lesson—one I hope I learned well enough not to repeat. I know I will work the story into a message on television, and hopefully it will help many others not to make the same mistake I made. Then what Satan meant for harm, God will turn for good (Genesis 50:20).

Procrastination

Intending to obey God later isn't obedience; it is procrastination, and it is a problem. Haggai 1:2–6 presents a good example of the kinds of problems procrastination causes. God had told the people to rebuild His house, but they kept putting it off while they built their own houses and allowed God's house to lie in ruins. They planted much but harvested little. They ate but never had enough. They put on clothes but were never warm. They earned wages only to put their money in a purse with holes in it. I am sure they were complaining, just as we do when our circumstances are not good, but God told them

> *Intending to obey God later isn't obedience; it is procrastination.*

to give "careful thought" to their ways and start building His house, as He had instructed them (Haggai 1:7–8). Haggai 1:2 in the Amplified Bible, Classic Edition says that God had told them to build His house eighteen years earlier. That's a long time to procrastinate and be disobedient.

Procrastination is deceptive because we tend to think planning to obey God equals obedience. But it doesn't. We have not obeyed until we have actually done what He asks us to do. Is there something in your life that you are putting off until another time? Do you need to forgive someone? Do you need to apologize to someone? Do you need to fulfill a promise you made to God? If so, I urge you to stop procrastinating and do it now.

God Is a Rewarder

God rewards those who obey Him. Even if we have done wrong and caused a mess, we can repent, change our mind for the better, go in the right direction, and still be blessed. One of the rewards we receive when we make godly choices is that we are completely satisfied (Matthew 5:6 AMPC). God rewards those who earnestly seek Him (Hebrews 11:6). God is a rewarder and His desire is to reward, not to punish. But because He loves us, He will correct us if that is the only way He can get our attention. We can learn to change

> God's desire is to reward, not to punish.

our ways before discipline is necessary if we will pay attention to God's Word and His Spirit.

Another way God rewards obedience is with answered prayer (1 John 3:22). Whoever listens to the Lord will "live in safety and be at ease, without fear of harm" (Proverbs 1:33). This doesn't mean that we will never have difficulty in our lives, but that God will deliver us from those difficulties in due time if we trust in Him.

Is it wrong to expect a reward for obeying God? Not at all, especially since He has promised it. Even though God has promised rewards, we still need to release our faith in order to receive them. God had to remind me recently that we cannot simply assume that His promises will automatically come to pass in our lives. We receive everything from God by faith, and faith is a force that needs to be released. It is released by praying, declaring God's Word, and/or taking God-inspired action. I am not suggesting we obey God only to get a reward. We should obey Him because we love and respect Him. But since He does promise rewards for obedience to Him, we should release our faith and ask Him for them.

> God is not unjust; he will not forget your work and the love you have shown him as you have helped his people and continue to help them.
>
> Hebrews 6:10

You may be thinking, *Joyce, do you mean that I can make a big mess out of my life and God will still bless me?* Yes, He absolutely will if you are sincerely repentant, take responsibility for your mess, and obey what He asks you to do to fix it. The apostle Peter denied knowing Christ, and he repented and went on to become one of the greatest apostles of Christ in all of history. Paul (formerly Saul) persecuted Christians, and after repentance, he served God wholeheartedly and wrote approximately two-thirds of the New Testament. The Bible is filled with people who made big messes out of their lives, but they took responsibility, repented, and ended up being blessed. The same can happen for you.

CHAPTER 3

Storms and Rainbows

The more you love rainbows the more you will have to bear with storms.

Matshona Dhliwayo[5]

Most of us love rainbows but don't like storms; however, rainbows appear only after rain or storms. A rainbow represents God's promise that the earth will never again be destroyed by a flood. He made this promise to Noah after the flood recorded in the Book of Genesis:

> I have set my rainbow in the clouds, and it will be the sign of the covenant between me and the earth. Whenever I bring clouds over the earth and the rainbow appears in the clouds, I will remember my covenant between me and you and all living creatures of every kind. Never again will the waters become a flood to destroy all life. Whenever the rainbow appears in the clouds, I will see it and remember the everlasting covenant between God and all living creatures of every kind on the earth.
>
> Genesis 9:13–16

Everyone faces storms in life—troubles, difficulties, painful situations, times of testing, and the like—from time to time. But there is a rainbow—symbolizing a blessing—at the end of every storm if we go through it God's way. But we do have to go through the storm to get to the blessing. David says to God in Psalm 23:4: "Even though I walk through the darkest valley, I will fear no evil, for you are with me." In this psalm David also says that God sets a table before him in the presence of his enemies and that his cup runs over (Psalm 23:5). He was being blessed right in the midst of the mess. When you are having trouble, don't just focus on the trouble, but also look for the blessings in your life.

Notice that David mentions walking *through* "the darkest valley." He was not delivered from it, but God was with him in it, and He blessed him.

I prayed many times for God to get me out of the childhood abuse by my father, but He didn't. However, He did take me through it, and I have come out victorious. Why didn't He deliver me? Only God knows the fullness of the answer to that question. But I do know that had He delivered me, I probably wouldn't be able to help as many people as I do now. My pain has been turned into gain for other people. I could have been bitter, and I was for many years, but I learned that God had a better plan. When I let go of the bitterness, He gave me something much better. He gave me blessing.

The healing I needed in my soul took quite a while, but God gave me the grace not to give up. As I mentioned previously, Isaiah 61:7 was one of the biblical promises I hung on to during that time: "You will rejoice in your inheritance. And so you will inherit a *double portion* in your land, and everlasting joy will be yours" (emphasis mine). I treasure this promise that God will give us a double blessing for our trouble and that He will give us joy.

I love to talk about God's promises, but it is also important to clarify what I mean when I say God will bless you in the midst of your mess if you do things His way. What is "His way"? An important and necessary part of His way is forgiving people who have hurt you. This is often extremely difficult to do. Why? Because often we don't think the people who hurt us deserve to be forgiven. But do we deserve the forgiveness that God graciously gives us? No, of course not. He is not asking us to do for others anything He doesn't do for us.

Even though your enemies may not deserve your forgiveness, you deserve peace, and you can give yourself peace by obeying God and trusting Him for the blessing you are due.

I had to forgive my father for abusing me and my mother for allowing the abuse, and I had to be willing to pray for and bless them. God asked me to take care of them in their old age, and although I didn't want to, I did it in obedience to Him. I now know that making sure they were well cared for was one of the most

> *Being good to someone who has hurt you disarms the devil.*

spiritually powerful things I have ever done. When you are good to someone who has really hurt you, it disarms the devil. He wants us to hate our enemies, but Jesus says to love them and be good to them: "But I say to you who hear, Love your enemies, do good to those who hate you, bless those who curse you, pray for those who abuse you" (Luke 6:27–28 ESV).

Like many other godly principles, forgiving and blessing those who have hurt us seems to make no sense. But when we are good to people when we don't think they deserve it, we are behaving as God does. Only God can give us the power to do this. I could not have taken care of my parents had He not given me the grace to do so.

One reason I am writing this book is so you will believe that at the end of every storm, you will find a rainbow (blessing). But I always have to add "if you do things God's way." Many people want God's blessings, but they don't want to obey Him, especially when He asks them to do something difficult.

How would you like to receive twice as much as you have lost? Most of us have had times when we really needed our friends to comfort us, but they found fault with us instead. If this has happened to you, be sure you pray for your friends so God can release a double blessing into your life. In the Old Testament story of Job, which I mentioned earlier, Job needed his friends to comfort him, but instead they accused him. He forgave them and prayed for them and God gave him twice as much as he had lost.

Start today believing God for a double blessing in your life, and ask Him if there is anything you need to do in order to release it. As long as we are bitter, we cannot get better. We must give up resentment, self-pity, unforgiveness, anger, and hatred and replace them with prayer and blessing. Trust God, and while you are trusting Him,

> You cannot get better when you are bitter.

do good (Psalm 37:3). Being a blessing to others when you are hurting is a powerful spiritual principle that defeats the devil. Romans 12:21 says that we "overcome evil with good."

Go Through

As I shared, God didn't deliver me from my situation, but He did take me through it. There are many times in life when we have to go through something difficult, but there will be a blessing at the end of it if we won't give up or refuse to obey God.

Hebrews 6:11, in the Amplified Bible, Classic Edition, says: "But we do [strongly and earnestly] desire for each of you to show the same diligence and sincerity [all the way through] in realizing and enjoying the full assurance and development of [your] hope until the end."

If we go through the difficult times that come our way, we will enjoy God's promised reward at the end. But if we run from them, we will not grow spiritually. We will probably have to take the test again, and we will miss the blessing God had in mind for us. Hebrews 11:6 (NKJV) teaches us that God blesses "those who diligently seek Him." Diligence is persistence in pressing forward no matter the circumstances that try to hinder us.

David had to go through the valley of the shadow of death, but he was blessed while his enemies watched (Psalm 23:4–5). Daniel had to go into the lions' den and spend the night trusting God that the lions would not eat him (Daniel 6:16). God sent an angel to shut the lions' mouths (Daniel 6:22). At the end of this story, King Darius was so impressed that he decreed that throughout his kingdom people had to fear and reverence the God that Daniel served (Daniel 6:26). When we Christians are threatened, we can be tempted to compromise due to fear of loss or fear of pain. But if we would hold firm, others who see our steadfastness and who are not believers might become believers. Then, instead of losing something, we would gain something more because of our refusal to compromise.

I have a personal example that drives home this point. I once worked for a company whose owners were not Christians. I was the bookkeeper, and part of my job was to send customers their statements at the end of the month so they would know how much they owed the company. One customer had accidently overpaid their account. The typical—and right—course of action would have been to send them a check for the overpayment, but my boss didn't want to do that.

He told me to debit their account for the amount of their credit and send them a statement indicating a zero balance. I knew that was wrong, and I went home and wrestled all night, trying to decide what to do. I had recently committed to $1,200 of dental work, and that was a *lot* of money. I felt I could not afford to lose my job. In addition to that, the location of my workplace made it easy for Dave to drop me off and pick me up because he worked in the same area, and we had only one car. As I pondered the situation, the upcoming dental expense and the convenience of my workplace were two big reasons I didn't want to lose my job. I was afraid that if I refused to do what my boss had asked me to do, he would fire me.

I didn't sleep well that night. I felt like I was in the lions' den with Daniel. After giving the situation much consideration, I knew I had to do the right thing. I decided that if I got fired, I would trust God to get me another job equal to or better than that one.

I went to work early the next morning, because my boss typically arrived early. I asked to speak to him, and said, "I am a Christian, and I cannot send the customer who overpaid their account a statement that makes us look as though we don't owe them money because I believe it would be wrong."

His face turned red with, I am sure, a mixture of anger and embarrassment. He simply told me to get back to work. He said nothing to me all day, and I fully expected him to come to my desk at any time and fire me. But God intervened and instead of firing me, my boss put the customer's statement faceup on my desk and told me to send them a check.

Within three years after that incident, I was gradually promoted to the point where I was second in charge of the company. The only person with more authority than I had was the boss himself. My decision made him respect me and know he could trust me. I thought I had a mess on my hands when the situation started, but God blessed me because I followed His principles of honesty and truth.

Always remember that if you do the right thing, even if you lose something initially because of your decision, in the end you will get a double blessing.

> *If you do the right thing, even if you lose something initially, in the end you will get a double blessing.*

Refuse to Compromise

In the Old Testament, Daniel could have avoided the lions' den by discontinuing his daily custom of praying to God three times a day, but he refused to compromise. He even prayed with his windows open because it was his normal habit. The king had ordered that for thirty days, people could not pray to anyone except him, but Daniel continued to pray to God, as he had previously (Daniel 6:1–10). Often, when we refuse to compromise our faith, it appears that we will suffer for our decision, but God always brings a blessing if we stand firm.

Before this story takes place in the Book of Daniel, three Hebrew men named Shadrach, Meshach, and Abed-Nego were thrown into a fiery furnace for refusing to worship a golden idol set up by King Nebuchadnezzar of Babylon (Daniel 3:10–18). During their time in that blazing furnace, a fourth man who looked like the "Son of God" was in the furnace with them (Daniel 3:24–25 NKJV). When the furnace door was opened, the king saw that no harm had come to them; they didn't even smell like smoke (Daniel 3:26–27). Nebuchadnezzar himself had seen the fourth man in the furnace, and I am convinced he knew that God had sent them supernatural help.

Another point I like to make about this story is that the Bible says Shadrach, Meshach, and Abed-Nego went into the furnace bound, but when the king saw them, they were loosed, or as Daniel 3:25 says "unbound and unharmed." I believe that when we go through difficulties, that is often when our bonds, the things that bind us, are broken off and we are set free.

> When you go through difficulties, that is when your bonds are broken.

When King Nebuchadnezzar saw how God saved Shadrach, Meshach, and Abed-Nego, he praised their God (Daniel 3:28). He also decreed that no one could say anything against their God, because no other god could save the way their God saved them (Daniel 3:29). In the end, Shadrach, Meshach, and Abed-Nego were promoted (Daniel 3:30). They went through the difficulty, and ultimately, they were blessed. I hope you are seeing the pattern of how God blesses those who stand firm through the storms of life and continue obeying Him.

Facing My Fears for My Family

Anne is a woman who endured many difficulties as a woman rooted in fear, but God kept blessing her even though she was a mess mentally and emotionally. She didn't give up. Her determination paid off, and now she is free. Here is her story:

> I love my kids. Many people do. But for a woman who didn't feel she had the skill set to be a nurturing, loving mom, this a good and glorious truth—a superpower even. You see, I grew up in an emotional storm. And I became one. I was deeply depressed, angry with myself, and bitter over the many disasters I had lived through.
>
> Through the years, I was blessed in many ways. I went to college and graduated. God spoke to my heart, and I became a Christian. After college, I got a great job in my area of study. Seven years later, I landed my dream job. God was blessing me in the midst of my mess, but I still saw all of the negative and none of the positive. I felt deeply inadequate and wanted to "be someone," not really believing that I already was "someone" whom God loved.
>
> I took all of my mess into a big blessing of a marriage, and then suddenly, God blessed me again. Almost like a strike of lightning, I became pregnant twice. Twenty-one months apart, two beautiful girls were born. No health problems. No complications. Two delightfully sweet babies with bright eyes and beautiful smiles.
>
> Even though I was an emotional wreck, I refused to see that my emotional condition was a choice I had made for myself. The

truth was, if I was willing, I could be healed and set free. That's what God wanted for me, but I saw myself as a high-functioning survivor who'd pulled herself up by her bootstraps all by herself. On the outside, my life looked mostly serene, but inside the storm was strong. And my husband was growing weary of chancy weather.

My daughters were very young, but they could still read the signs. They needed security, not sudden storms. They needed a peaceful, stable home in which they could thrive. I finally reached the point where I was ready to stop making apologies and start improving my behavior.

As I became willing to change, God set me free. As I agreed with His Word and let go of my past hurts, He healed me. As I humbled myself, He lifted me. As I chose faith over fear, He cheered me on. As I spoke aloud what He wanted for me and for my family, He came through for me.

Today, I am able to trust God for His love, joy, peace, patience, kindness, goodness, faithfulness, gentleness, and self-control (Galatians 5:22–23 ESV). My daughters have a mom who enjoys being a mom. Rather than being fearful that I'm not cut out for the job, I'm even grateful for the challenges motherhood brings because I know God will help me. His unconditional love is something I will never have to live without. I still make mistakes, and I always will, but I know God will work out everything for my good. There is nothing He wouldn't do for me in the middle of my mess. And there's nothing He won't do for you in the middle of yours.

Paul and Silas in Prison

The early believers faced many difficulties, but the good attitude they maintained while going through them often caused others to believe too. I think the same would happen today if we would keep a good attitude through our struggles and be strong enough spiritually not to back away from difficulties.

Paul and Silas encountered a female slave who practiced divination (an occult means of uncovering hidden knowledge, similar to fortune-telling). As she followed Paul and Silas, she shouted, "These men are servants of the Most High God, who are telling you the way to be saved" (Acts 16:17). Even though she spoke truth, she irritated Paul because she was drawing attention to herself and spoke out of a wrong spirit. Paul put up with her for a period of time, but eventually he became so annoyed that he turned to her and commanded the evil spirit to come out of her in the name of Jesus Christ (Acts 16:18). At his command the spirit did come out, and her owners were upset because she had made them a lot of money when this spirit was operating through her (Acts 16:18–19). They captured Paul and Silas and dragged them into the marketplace to face the city authorities, saying, "These men are Jews, and are throwing our city into an uproar by advocating customs unlawful for us Romans to accept or practice" (Acts 16:20–21).

The magistrates ordered Paul and Silas to be stripped, beaten with rods, and thrown into prison (Acts 16:22–23). Before we go any further, stop and think about how they may have felt or what they may have thought. They were doing God's will and found themselves beaten and in prison. At this point, they could have developed a bad attitude and been bitter and resentful. Instead, behind their prison doors, they were praying and singing hymns at midnight (Acts 16:25).

The jailer had been instructed to guard them carefully, so he had put them in the inner cell and fastened their feet in stocks (Acts 16:23–24). While they were praying and singing, the other prisoners listened (Acts 16:25). Acts 16:26–30 reveals what happened next:

> Suddenly there was such a violent earthquake that the foundations of the prison were shaken. At once all the prison doors flew open, and everyone's chains came loose. The jailer woke up, and when he saw the prison doors open, he drew his sword and was about to kill himself because he thought the prisoners had escaped. But Paul shouted, "Don't harm yourself! We are all here!" The jailer called for lights, rushed in and fell trembling before Paul and Silas. He then brought them out and asked, "Sirs, what must I do to be saved?"

What an amazing story! Because Paul and Silas remained stable, persevered, trusted God, and went through their difficulty with a good attitude, their actions caused the jailer to want to serve their God. This is certainly a blessing that came from a storm. I think we will all find blessings from the storms we go through in life if we handle them God's way.

CHAPTER 4

Overcoming Tests, Trials, and Temptations

Trials should not surprise us, or cause us to doubt God's faithfulness. Rather, we should actually be glad for them. God sends trials to strengthen our trust in him so that our faith will not fail. Our trials keep us trusting; they burn away our self-confidence and drive us to our Savior.

Edmund Clowney[6]

Part of the Christian life involves increasing in our faith and trust in God and growing stronger as believers. This often happens through times of trial and testing. One of the blessings God brings from our struggles is the ability to help others as a result of what we have been through. In order to help people, there are times when we must personally go through difficulties and messes so we will truly understand and have compassion on them. We can rest in God if we will only believe that when trouble comes to us, we will be stronger when it is over.

Dealing with difficulty is like lifting weights in the gym. When I started working out with a trainer, I could only bench press ten pounds. After a while, he gave me twelve and a half pounds. At first, that amount of weight felt heavy, but soon it wasn't any more difficult than the ten pounds. I then graduated to fifteen pounds, then to seventeen and a half, then to twenty and eventually to twenty-two and a half pounds. I use this example to show that we can handle more and more if it is added gradually. God knows what we can handle, and His Word promises that He will never bring more on us than we can bear (1 Corinthians 10:13).

> *Dealing with difficulty is like lifting weights in the gym.*

Twenty-two and a half pounds may not sound like much to you, but it was a lot for me since I was about sixty-five years old when I did it. Each time they added weight, I thought I couldn't lift it, but with encouragement, I did. Our walk with God is the same way. When He allows difficulties in our lives, He is actually making us stronger and preparing us for the future.

A good example of what I'm talking about is that in the beginning of our ministry we needed just a little money to run it. I worried constantly about where the funds would come from and often felt afraid they wouldn't come in at all. As the ministry grew little by little, we needed more and more money to pay the employees and the bills. My faith gradually grew stronger as I went through situations and experienced God's faithfulness, but it took years for me to grow to the point where I could trust God and not worry about where the money would come from. Now, the expense involved in being on television in two-thirds of the world and paying a staff of more than five hundred people is staggering, and I never even think about it. I am assured that if God wants me to do what I am doing, He will provide everything we need in order to do it. If He ever doesn't want me to do it, then I am happy to do something else if that is what He wants. After many years, I finally know that my worth and value are not in what I do, but in who I am in Christ.

Every time we needed more money for the ministry God used it as a test to see if I could remain peaceful and trust Him to provide. Just as schoolchildren must pass tests before they are promoted to the next grade, we are tested before progressing to the next level in our ministries.

Jesus told Peter that Satan wanted to sift him like wheat, and that when the experience was over, Peter would be able to strengthen the people around him. The enemy, Satan, wanted to shake Peter's faith, hoping to destroy it. But Jesus, wanting Peter to become stronger, prayed that his faith would not fail (Luke 22:31–32). Similarly, Jesus prays for us as we experience tests, trials, and temptations (John 17:9; Romans 8:34).

When the devil tries to shake your faith hoping to destroy it, remember that God is trying to give you a promotion. Your job is to remain steady, keep trusting Him, continue walking in love with people and helping those in need, and stay positive. The test will eventually end, and you will be stronger than you were before, ready for the greater thing God has for you.

When you are in the midst of the difficulty, remembering that it will come to an end and that you will be blessed can be a challenge. But these assurances will help you go through the difficulty without giving up.

Another way to help yourself through a hard situation is to remember that you are not the only one going through such difficulties. First Peter 5:9 teaches us that we are to remember that our fellow believers in other parts of the world are suffering and passing through the same experiences we face.

Our trials test us and even tempt us to disobey God and give up on serving Him. The devil will do anything he can to prevent us from loving and serving God, but we will always be able to resist him as long as we stay close to God and follow His guidance.

Tests Come on the Road to Fulfilled Promises

When God called Abram (later Abraham) to eventually become the father of faith, He told him that if he obeyed Him, He would make him into a great nation, bless him, and make him a blessing (Genesis 12:2). But Abram experienced many trials and tests of his faith before he saw the complete fulfillment of God's promise. God called him to do something great, but he had to be prepared for what God had prepared for him. I experienced something similar.

God spoke to my heart in 1976 about teaching His Word all over the world, but it was at least thirty years before I saw the complete fulfillment of what He had said. During that time, I grew spiritually, and the ministry grew in reaching greater numbers of people. But there were many trials and tests along the way.

I wish I could tell you that if you pass a test once, you will never have to go through it again, but I wouldn't be telling you the truth. I believe we will be tested from time to time as long as we are in our flesh-and-bone bodies. The more experience we have, the easier the tests are to pass, but we will still face them. Occasionally the devil will throw something at us that we haven't experienced before, and it may shake us like nothing ever has, but God will bring us through it and give us victory. Don't be afraid when you have to confront things that are new to you. God will guide you through the challenge and bring you out with more experience, strength, faith, and wisdom than you had previously.

> *Don't be afraid to confront things that are new to you.*

Think again about lifting weights. When I reach a certain point of strength, as long as I continue to work out with weights, I will maintain it. But if I stop, I will lose the strength I've gained. Likewise, our faith may become strong as a result of being tested, but if it's not tested again, it may weaken, even to the point where it would cave in through the smallest difficulty. Faith must be used in order to remain strong, and difficulty forces us to use our faith.

Often, when I ask people how they are, they tell me about something they are "going through." I am tempted to say, "Well, thank God you are 'going through' and not stuck in the middle of it." Things could be a lot worse than going through something difficult. Just imagine all the people in the world who have huge problems and don't know Jesus. Now, *that* would be hard. With Jesus, we always have hope, but without Him, people are without hope. As we go through difficulties, we have assurance they will eventually end and that we will be stronger spiritually when we get to the other side of them.

> *You will be stronger when you get to the other side of your difficulties.*

From Test to Testimony

Allowing your test to become your testimony can help you reach people who don't know Jesus. If they see what God has done for you, they may also believe He might do it for them.

Hundreds of people have told me that, after hearing my testimony, they thought, *If she can make it through what she went through, then there is hope for me.* My test became my testimony; my mess became my miracle and my message. I have experienced the double blessing mentioned in Isaiah 61:7: "Instead of your shame you will receive a double portion, and instead of disgrace you will rejoice in your inheritance. And so you will inherit a double portion in your land, and everlasting joy will be yours."

> A mess may become your miracle and your message.

We all get tested, but not everyone ends up with a testimony of victory. People who refuse to let trials do their work will get to take the tests over again. I have discovered that in God's school, we never fail; we just keep taking the same tests until we pass them.

If you are going through something difficult, why not benefit from it instead of just being miserable and not ending up any better off? Pass your test and get it over with. God doesn't rejoice in our sufferings, but He does rejoice when we endure them by trusting Him and maintaining a good attitude.

> In God's school, you never fail.

Suffering

It is evident that the world is full of suffering. Physical, emotional, and mental pain have been and always will be an intrinsic part of the human experience. The example of our suffering is Jesus

Christ, who was persecuted and crucified for our sins. Suffering will indeed come, but God can give us grace and power to overcome every trial and to fulfill our purpose and mission in His kingdom, and He can work something good out of it. Through suffering, we gain experience that enables us to help others, we grow spiritually, and we develop godly character. Romans 5:3–4 says: "Not only so, but we also glory in our sufferings, because we know that suffering produces perseverance; perseverance, character; and character, hope."

> Through suffering, you grow spiritually.

Spiritual growth is one of the most important things we can seek. Paul writes about "infants in Christ" and mature ones in 1 Corinthians 3:1–2:

> Brothers and sisters, I could not address you as people who live by the Spirit but as people who are still worldly—mere infants in Christ. I gave you milk, not solid food, for you were not yet ready for it. Indeed, you are still not ready.

When people are still in the infant stage of Christianity, it can be difficult to talk to them about trials, tests, temptations, and suffering. Like a baby, they just want to play and have a good time. They want to hear messages that make them feel better—messages of God's love for them, His good plan for them, the blessings they can look forward to in the future, and similarly uplifting truths. These messages are certainly important, as we all need to know that God loves us and has good plans for our lives, but they are part of a bigger picture of the Christian life, which does include suffering at times.

Paul refers to these feel-good messages as "milk," stating that the infant believers were not ready for "solid food." I often refer to these messages as "dessert" and tell people that while dessert may be enjoyable, we cannot only eat dessert and be healthy. We need the messages that encourage us and make us feel good, but we also need spiritual meat and vegetables. In other words, we cannot grow spiritually, become strong, and be transformed into the image of Jesus Christ without learning to love messages that help us grow, even if they aren't as tasty as dessert.

Messages that are what I would call "solid food" are ones about personal sacrifice, serving others, enduring suffering in order to do God's will, enduring persecution for the sake of the gospel, going through trials and tests with a good attitude, giving, and other important topics that help us grow. It is important for Christians who want to grow spiritually to hear a healthy balance of different kinds of teaching. If we only hear messages that make us feel good, we won't grow spiritually. But if we only hear messages that correct us, we will become discouraged and want to give up. We need the whole counsel of God's Word.

Since Christ suffered in the flesh for us, we should arm ourselves "with the same thought and purpose [patiently to suffer rather than fail to please God]." If we will do this, we will no longer sin intentionally and we won't live to please ourselves, but God (1 Peter 4:1–2 AMPC).

What kind of suffering might one encounter? I will use my personal example, and maybe you will relate to it. As I have said, I was a mess when I began my relationship with God through Christ. Once I became serious about wanting to grow spiritually, I asked God to do whatever needed to be done in me for me to become the kind of person He could use and be pleased with.

I suffered "in the flesh" (meaning that I felt mental and emotional pain) as I learned how to submit to my husband Dave's authority, because men had abused me in the past. I suffered in the flesh while learning to be willing to admit I was wrong when Dave and I had a disagreement over something. It was hard for me not to have the last word in an argument or not to get my way in everything from how we decorated our home to choosing a restaurant if we planned to eat out. I suffered when people I trusted betrayed me.

God calls us to walk according to His Spirit and not according to our flesh (Galatians 5:16–17). In other words, we are to do what God leads us to do, not what our flesh wants to do. This process takes time, practice, and the renewing of our mind. As we learn to think differently, walking by the Spirit becomes easier.

Colossians 3:5 says, "Put to death, therefore, whatever belongs to your earthly nature." The Amplified Bible indicates that "put to death" means "deprive of power," teaching us that we are to deprive our flesh of the power to rule us. In the natural world, anything can be put to death if it is not fed and nourished. Our fleshly nature is no different. Every time we give in to the desires of our flesh, we feed our fleshly nature; and each time we deprive it of the power to rule us, we don't feed it. If we deprive our flesh for long enough, it will die. In other words, its power over us will be weakened to the point where it is no longer a problem in the area we are addressing.

> When you give in to the desires of the flesh, you feed your fleshly nature.

First Peter 3:14 says that if we suffer for what is right, we are blessed. For example, God's Word teaches us to live in peace (Romans 12:18; Colossians 3:15). If someone treats me unjustly and everything in me wants to confront them, but I know it will just make the situation worse and probably blow up into a huge argument, I would be wise to cast the care of that situation onto God and let Him be my vindicator. But to do that, my flesh would not get its way, and therefore I would suffer, in a way, to do what is right. My flesh would hate waiting, but the outcome would be good.

We deal with difficult situations frequently, and each one is a test for us and an opportunity to practice not feeding our flesh. As

> You will grow stronger as you follow God's will.

we follow God's will, we will grow stronger and God will be able to use us in greater ways.

No Parking in Your Pain

Over the years, I've spoken with many people who allowed their pain or hardships to keep them from moving forward. I call this "parking in your pain." Painful experiences can leave us bitter, offended, and focused on the person or situation that has harmed us. But we have another choice. We can move past the pain—we can forgive anyone who has hurt us, and we can let God deal with the situation. Ask God to heal your brokenness and your wounds. Put yourself in His hands and follow His guidance, and you will see God turn your mess into a blessing.

Psalm 37:1–3 gives us great advice: "Do not fret because of those who are evil or be envious of those who do wrong; for like the grass they will soon wither, like green plants they will soon die away. Trust in the Lord and do good; dwell in the land and enjoy safe pasture."

We don't need to worry about all the evil and people who do evil in the world because they won't last. We should simply trust God and keep doing what is good—and we will enjoy safety and blessing.

Life is not fair, and not everything that happens to us is fair, but God is just, meaning that He makes wrong things right at the proper time. As you place your trust in Him and do things His way, He will reward you many times over and use your difficulties for your good.

You and I may never fully understand everything that happens in our lives until we get to heaven (where we will fully understand), but God doesn't ask us to understand; He asks us to trust Him. Focus on trusting Him and everything will work out right in the end. You will have blessings instead of messes in your life.

> God asks you to trust Him.

PART 2

Living a Blessed Life

CHAPTER 5

Choose to Be Blessed

And I will make of you a great nation, and I will bless you [with abundant increase of favors] and make your name famous and distinguished, and you will be a blessing [dispensing good to others].

Genesis 12:2 AMPC

When God created human beings, He never wanted our lives to become a mess. He didn't intend for us to live miserable, frustrated lives filled with trouble and tragedy. His intent has always been for us to live a blessed life and to be a blessing to others. However, when Adam and Eve chose to disobey the one command He gave them in the Garden of Eden—not to eat of the tree of the knowledge of good and evil—sin entered into the entire human race (Genesis 2:16–17; 3:6–7; Romans 5:12), and with it came every kind of misery that sin brings.

Jesus came to redeem us from sin (Ephesians 1:7). Therefore, the blessed way of living life that God originally intended for us is still available. We simply have to choose it on a regular basis. The Bible is filled with scriptures that teach us about the blessed life (Deuteronomy 28:3–6; 2 Corinthians 9:8; Ephesians 1:3). In this chapter, we want to look at some of them and be sure we are doing what we need to do in order to enjoy a life of blessing. Let's start with Psalm 1:1–4 (ESV):

> Blessed is the man who walks not in the counsel of the wicked, nor stands in the way of sinners, nor sits in the seat of scoffers; but his delight is in the law of the Lord, and on his law he meditates day and night. He is like a tree planted by streams of water that yields its fruit in its season, and its leaf does not wither. In all that he does, he prospers. The wicked are not so, but are like chaff that the wind drives away.

This Scripture passage emphasizes the importance of the type of people we spend our time with and warns us against taking counsel from the wicked, meaning the ungodly. Let me ask you: What kind of people do you spend your time with? Do they help you grow in godliness? Do they encourage you in your faith? Where do you turn when you need advice? Do you seek help from God first and people who know and honor God's Word, or do you consult sources that will not give you godly counsel?

Some people look for advice from fortune tellers, mediums, or psychics, but God forbids these practices. We read about this in Leviticus 19:31, in Isaiah 8:19, and in this passage from Deuteronomy 18:10–12:

> Let no one be found among you who sacrifices their son or daughter in the fire, who practices divination or sorcery, interprets omens, engages in witchcraft, or casts spells, or who is a medium or spiritist or who consults the dead. Anyone who does these things is detestable to the Lord; because of these same detestable practices the Lord your God will drive out those nations before you.

Astrology has become popular among many people. They consult their horoscope daily and even chart their lives by the stars before they make decisions. But God's Word forbids His people to practice astrology (Deuteronomy 4:19; Isaiah 47:13–14). Why should we consult the stars when we can communicate with the One who made them?

Choose Your Friends Wisely

I cannot count the number of people I have heard or read about who say their lives are in a mess because they have gotten involved with individuals who are not good for them or they have hung around with a bad crowd. It is important that we choose godly

people for friends, especially as our close friends. Psalm 1:1 says
that those who are blessed do not interact closely with sinners
or mockers. A mocker is someone who makes fun of someone or
something. Sometimes they make
fun of religion or moral values. In
terms of "sinners," we all sin. Everyone has sin in their life, but that is

> You should choose godly
> people as your friends.

different from living a lifestyle of intentional, habitual sin, which
I believe is what Psalm 1 counsels us against.

I would add that we should not be in close relationship with
gossipers (those who tell other people's secrets, also called "tale-
bearers" [Proverbs 20:19 NKJV, AMPC]), those who are judgmental,
or people who are negative. Proverbs 23:20–21 also teaches us
not to associate with drunkards or gluttons. We often pick up the
habits of those we spend a lot of time with, so choosing our asso-
ciates carefully is important. We don't want to completely avoid
relationships with people who are not believers, because we want
to be a witness to them. My advice is to spend time with them as
long as you are *affecting* them and they are not *infecting* you.

Delight yourself in God's Word and meditate on it day and
night (Psalm 1:2). Spend a lot of time studying, listening to, and
reading God's Word, because it reveals God's will and the way to
the blessed life.

People who live by the precepts of Psalm 1 will be stable, like
a tree planted by the water; they will bring forth good fruit, and
all they do will prosper (Psalm 1:3). Based on years of study, I
would define *prosperity* to mean "to do well." It refers to more than
money; it is an ongoing state of success that touches every area of
our lives. I think the word *prosper* is simply another way of saying God wants us to live a blessed life. I have read that Jewish
thinkers thought that *blessed* meant to increase in joy and peace-
fulness, and I suppose this is because one of the Hebrew words

for *blessed*—the word *esher*, used in Psalm 1—means "happiness."[7] (Strong's 835).

If you want to be successful, follow the instructions in Joshua 1:8 (ESV):

> This Book of the Law shall not depart from your mouth, but you shall meditate on it day and night, so that you may be careful to do according to all that is written in it. For then you will make your way prosperous, and then you will have good success.

Spiritual prosperity is more important than material prosperity and should always be sought before anything else. There is certainly nothing wrong with being financially blessed. Having money is good, as long as money doesn't have us. Without money, we cannot give financially to the work of the Lord, and being generous protects us from becoming greedy.

> *Spiritual prosperity is more important than material prosperity.*

The first and most important key to living a blessed life is always to put God first in everything. The first and most important commandment is to love God with all your heart, soul, and mind (Matthew 22:37–38), and the first of the Ten Commandments states, "You shall have no other gods before me" (Exodus 20:3). God should be first in our thoughts, conversation, priorities, the way we spend our time, and the distribution of our finances. Don't worship your career, a sport, fame, or wealth. Worship God.

Obedience Leads to Blessing

If we truly want to live the blessed life, we must obey God to the best of our ability. Deuteronomy 28:1 says: "If you fully obey the

Lord your God and carefully follow all his commands I give you today, the Lord your God will set you high above all the nations on earth." Jesus says that if we love Him, we will obey Him (John 14:15). Obedience to God is not always the most popular subject these days, because the world is filled with rebellious people who want to go their own way. They certainly have a right to make that choice, but I can assure you that they will not be happy with the outcome of such a life. I watched my father live that kind of life, and at the end of it, even though he was born again three years before he died, he still had nothing but regrets.

God's ways are best. Everything He tells us to do or not to do is for our benefit. He tells us what we need to know so things will work out best for us and lead us into the blessed life. People have historically said "God bless you" when someone in their presence sneezes, but I can assure you that God wants to bless us far beyond a mere sneeze. Look at what 1 Kings 2:3 says: "Observe what the Lord your God requires: Walk in obedience to him, and keep his decrees and commands, his laws and regulations, as written in the Law of Moses. Do this *so that you may prosper in all you do and wherever you go*" (emphasis mine).

The Bible teaches us to stay on the narrow path that leads to life and to stay off the broad path that leads to destruction (Matthew 7:13). On the narrow path, there is no room for what I call our "fleshly baggage." It isn't a road where we can do just what we want to do, but one on which we follow Jesus and do what He would do and what He has asked us to do.

There are many instructions in God's Word about what to do and what not to do. What we *believe* is important, but what we *do* is also important, because in the long run what we do proves what we believe.

When a Pharisee asked Jesus what the most important commandment was, He answered:

> " 'Love the Lord your God with all your heart and with all your soul and with all your mind.' This is the first and greatest commandment. And the second is like it: 'Love your neighbor as yourself.' "
>
> Matthew 22:37–39

Loving God is usually easier than loving people, because He is always good, and people are not. People hurt us, abuse us, disappoint us, betray us, and affect us negatively in many ways. Yet Jesus tells us to forgive them as He has forgiven us (Matthew 6:12–14; Mark 11:25) and to love even our enemies (Luke 6:27–35).

Forgiveness is God's commandment, but many people ignore it. This is unwise, because if we don't forgive, we forfeit the blessed life Jesus died for us to have. In fact, Jesus even says that if we don't forgive our enemies their trespasses, then God won't forgive ours (Matthew 6:15).

I suspect that, in the world, there are more people who are angry with someone than are not. This gives Satan an open door to work in their lives. Paul teaches us in his letter to the Ephesians that we are not to let the sun go down on our anger, or we will give the devil a foothold in our lives (Ephesians 4:26–27). He teaches us in 2 Corinthians 2:10–11 to forgive in order to keep Satan from getting an advantage over us. When I look at these verses, it seems to me that

> *Do not let the sun go down on your anger.*

we do ourselves—not our enemies—a favor when we choose to forgive. We protect ourselves from attacks by the devil through being obedient to God in this matter.

If you are having a difficult time forgiving someone, let me suggest a few things to consider:

- God does not ask us to forgive our enemies for any more than He forgives us.
- Forgiveness is not a feeling; it is a decision to treat people as Jesus would treat them.
- We are told to love our enemies and pray for those who persecute us (Matthew 5:44). This helps us forgive them. It is hard to pray for someone regularly and also stay angry with them.
- God is our Vindicator, and when we pray for our enemies, we put them in His hands.
- Even if our enemies don't deserve our forgiveness, we deserve peace. Forgiveness brings us peace.
- Only loving those who love you in return is not hard, but loving those who have hurt you is Christlike.
- If your enemy is in need, help him. Nothing does more damage to Satan's kingdom than for us to love and help our enemies.
- Remember, Jesus says, "Love your enemies, do good to those who hate you, bless those who curse you, pray for those who mistreat you" (Luke 6:27–28).

Obey God, Not People

We cannot be people-pleasers and God-pleasers at the same time.

You cannot be a people-pleaser and a God-pleaser at the same time.

When the authorities in Jerusalem told Peter and the apostles with him to stop preaching in Jesus' name, they answered, "We must obey God rather than human beings!" (Acts 5:29). And Paul wrote in Galatians 1:10 that if he had been trying to be popular with people, he would not have been a servant of

Christ. Our reputation in heaven is much more important than our reputation on earth.

Obedience requires sacrifice. We often have to sacrifice other people's approval in order to have God's approval. This requires learning to live unselfishly, and we learn unselfishness progressively, little by little. We will probably be learning to be more and more unselfish for as long as we live.

In order to obey God, we often need to sacrifice what we want in favor of what He wants. Although this may seem hard to do, the joy we receive from knowing we are in God's will is worth it. There is no harder pillow to try to sleep on than a guilty conscience.

> *There is no harder pillow than a guilty conscience.*

Even those of us who truly want to obey God will make mistakes, and we thank God for His forgiveness. His mercies are new every morning (Lamentations 3:22–23). Not only does He mercifully forgive us, but there is no condemnation for those who are in Christ (Romans 8:1). We don't have to waste days feeling guilty; we only need to repent, receive God's gracious forgiveness, and go on living our life in obedience to Him, enjoying the blessings He graciously gives.

Freedom from Selfishness

Jesus says that to be His disciples we must deny ourselves and lay down our life for others (Matthew 16:24–25). We are all called upon to die to self (John 12:24–25). In other words, we must be willing to give up what we want in favor of doing what God wants. Max Lucado says, "God loves us too much to indulge our every whim."[8] If you live your life as though everything is about you, that's all you'll be left with—you!

Jesus died that we might no longer live to and for ourselves, but to and for Him (2 Corinthians 5:15 AMPC). To be set free from self

> To be free from self is the
> greatest freedom.

is truly the greatest freedom we can have. It is wonderful to not get your way and still be content and happy.

Don't settle for a life that is anything other than blessed. Don't buy into the doctrine that to be a Christian you must be miserable and have nothing. Nothing in Scripture supports that idea. Yes, we will make sacrifices, but when making them for the will of God, we can do so joyfully. We can be content whether we have a lot or a little (Philippians 4:11–12), but if we handle faithfully the little bit we do have, God says He will give us more (Matthew 25:23).

Part of being faithful over what God has given us is to be generous in giving to others. Don't forget the poor, because they are very important to God. God not only told Abram He would bless him, but He told him that He would make him a blessing (Genesis 12:2). Ask God to bless you so you can bless others.

Right behavior begins with right thinking, and the Bible says that we should take captive our thoughts to make them obedient to Jesus Christ (2 Corinthians 10:5).

If you still have any doubt that God wants you to live a good and blessed life, consider this scripture:

> For we are God's [own] handiwork (His workmanship), recreated in Christ Jesus, [born anew] that we may do those good works which God predestined (planned beforehand) for us [taking paths which He prepared ahead of time], that we should walk in them [living the good life which He prearranged and made ready for us to live].
>
> Ephesians 2:10 AMPC

Notice that God has prearranged a "good life," and it is ready for us to live if we will be obedient to Him.

CHAPTER 6

Don't Be Offended by Trouble

If you're constantly being hurt, offended, or angered, you should honestly evaluate your inflamed ego.

Brant Hansen[9]

Jesus tells a parable about a farmer who was sowing some seed (Mark 4:3–9, 14–20). The farmer represents the Holy Spirit, and the seed symbolizes the Word of God. In the parable, Jesus speaks about the ground into which the seed is sown, and the ground represents the different conditions of people's hearts.

When some people hear God's Word, Satan, our enemy, comes immediately to take away that message (v. 15). This would be like a seed that blows away before it can take root in the ground. The enemy may do this in a variety of ways. For example, Satan loves to distract us when we are trying to study God's Word so we will not focus on what it teaches us. Or maybe we hear the Word but soon lose our temper, become angry, and forget what we heard. Or maybe we hear the Word and forget it quickly for some other reason. The ways that Satan devises to steal the Word from us are too many to count.

Jesus also speaks of seed sown in rocky ground (v. 16). This represents people who receive and welcome God's Word with joy, but they only endure for a little while because they don't allow the Word to go deep into their hearts. When trouble or persecution arises because of the Word, "they immediately are offended (become displeased, indignant, resentful), and they stumble and fall away" from its teaching (v. 17 AMPC).

People who have inflated egos often become indignant when they have trouble. They may encourage those who are struggling and tell them to trust God, but if difficulty happens to them, they are offended. Even though they don't see themselves this way, they think they are superior to or more spiritually mature than others and thus they should not have the troubles other people have.

The English word *offense* comes from the Greek word *skandalon*. This describes the part of a trap on which the bait hangs to lure the animal into the trap. If you are trying to catch a fish, you put some type of bait on the fish hook. If you are trying to catch a mouse, you put cheese or something else a mouse might bite on the trap. Satan uses a similar tactic. He baits us with offense, hoping to draw us into a full-blown case of bitterness, resentment, unforgiveness, or some other negative response.

Life offers us many opportunities to become offended, but the Bible tells us not to take offense and become angry (James 1:19–20 AMPC). If someone offered us poison, we would not take it, and offense, resentment, unforgiveness, indignation, and bitterness all poison our spiritual life. They poison our attitudes and steal our joy and peace. When the enemy tempts us to give in to these spiritual poisons, we should not partake of them.

An offense is also considered a stumbling block, something we trip and fall over. God is referred to as a rock in relation to believers and unbelievers. To believers, He is the rock of our salvation (2 Samuel 22:47 AMP), but to unbelievers, He is a rock of offense (1 Peter 2:7–8 AMP) that they trip over and fall to their ruin. People can either put their faith in God and receive eternal life, or they can stumble over Him and face eternal judgment.

People may refer to themselves as Christians and go to church. Everything in life may go along fine for them until God's Word confronts behavior they are unwilling to give up. At that point, Jesus becomes a stumbling stone to them. They fall away, or as we often say, they backslide.

I think we would be surprised to know how many people are angry with God because of a painful situation for which they blame Him. They simply don't understand how or why God could allow such circumstances to happen to them. I heard a sermon illustration about a man whose son had cancer, and although the man and many other people prayed for the boy to be healed, he died. The man became angry with God and said to Him, "Where were You when my son died?" God answered and said, "The same place I was when mine died."

We don't understand why bad things happen to good people, why young people die, or why certain people suffer with sickness and disease. I don't claim to have the answers to these difficult situations, but I have made the choice to trust God even when I don't understand certain circumstances, because I know that He is good and works all things out for the good of those who love Him (Romans 8:28). You will see Romans 8:28 mentioned several times in this book because I believe it helps us understand one of the ways God blesses us in the messes of our lives. He doesn't *do* bad things, but He can *use* them and work good from them. I have said many times, "There is no such thing as trusting God if we have no unanswered questions." We trust

> You cannot trust God if you have no unanswered questions.

God because we *don't* have the answers and we cannot solve our own problems.

The Bible tells us that God's ways are past finding out:

> Oh, the depth of the riches both of the wisdom and knowledge of God! How unsearchable are His judgments and His ways past finding out!
>
> Romans 11:33 NKJV

Let's consider again the parable in Mark 4. When Christians become offended, indignant, and resentful, they stumble and fall away from faith in God. These believers have no root, and when they have trouble because of the Word, they are immediately offended. According to Mark 4:17 (AMP):

> They have no real root in themselves, so they endure only for a little while; then, when trouble or persecution comes because of the word, immediately they [are offended and displeased at being associated with Me and] stumble and fall away.

This is a good place to take a short break and ask yourself how you handle trouble. What is the attitude of your heart when you face difficulty? Do you become angry with God, or do you trust Him? Are you offended when you have trials and tribulations, or do you realize

Your trials can make you a better person or a bitter one.

they are part of life and everyone has to deal with them? Our trials can make us better people, or they can drive us to become bitter and fall away from God.

Mark 4:17 tells us that trouble and persecution come because of God's Word. Satan attacks us, hoping to prevent us from learning and growing spiritually in the Word. He hopes trouble and persecution will cause us to doubt God's goodness and think we cannot trust Him.

Putting Down Roots

Notice that Mark 4:17 says that those who fall away during times of trouble and persecution have no roots. Think of a large oak tree. Dave and I have one in our backyard, and it is probably fifty years old or older. It has deep roots, and when storms come, they never destroy that tree. Its branches and leaves may blow around or even break occasionally, but the tree itself stands firm.

God's Word says that we are to become "oaks of righteousness, the planting of the Lord, that he may be glorified" (Isaiah 61:3 ESV). God is glorified when we stand firm and trust Him during the trials in our lives. When you face trouble, remember to keep obeying God and trusting Him to show you what to do or to remove the problem somehow.

God told the Israelites that He led them through the wilderness to humble them and test them, to see if they would keep His commandments:

> Remember how the Lord your God led you all the way in the wilderness these forty years, to humble and test you in order to know what was in your heart, whether or not you would keep his commands. He humbled you, causing you to hunger and then feeding you with manna, which neither you nor your ancestors had known, to teach you that man does not live on bread alone but on every word that comes from the mouth of the Lord.
>
> Deuteronomy 8:2–3

During their journey through the wilderness, God sent a special food called manna for the Israelites to eat (Exodus 16:4–35). It came from heaven one day at a time, teaching the Israelites to trust God to provide for them each day. They were not allowed to gather more manna than they needed for one day, except on the day before the Sabbath, because it did not fall on the Sabbath day. Each day they had to trust God that more manna would come the next day. Although we want to know what the future will bring, like the Israelites, we must learn to trust God one day at a time.

Many people today are like the Israelites long ago; they are tempted to complain and grumble when they encounter hardships. During the forty years God led the Israelites through the wilderness, they experienced many difficulties, and their response was to murmur, complain, and blame God and Moses (Exodus 15:24; 17:3–4; Numbers 14:2, 27). On one occasion, while the Israelites were waiting for Moses to come down from Mount Sinai, where he was meeting with God and receiving the Ten Commandments, they became impatient and made a golden calf and worshipped it (Exodus 32:1–6).

The Israelites' response to trials and tribulation was not positive, and we should learn from them. Of all the people delivered from bondage in Egypt, only two of the original group—Joshua and Caleb—entered the Promised Land. That's not a very good percentage, considering that six hundred thousand men, plus women and children, originally left Egypt with Moses (Exodus 12:37).

If we desire to experience the fulfillment of God's promises, we will have to not be like the Israelites during their time of testing. We can learn from them if we will, and we can choose not to repeat the behavior they displayed. Their pattern was to murmur, complain, and blame until things became so difficult that they realized they had sinned. Then they would finally repent of their sin and God would once again bless them. After a while, they would return to murmuring, complaining, and blaming. They repeated this process throughout their forty years of wandering. Their journey through the wilderness should have taken only eleven days, but God took them the long, hard route because He knew that if they reached the Promised Land and saw the war they would have to face to take possession of it (faced difficulty), they would turn and run.

The shortest, easiest way through a situation is not always the best way. The Israelites needed roots, and the only way for them to get them was for God to take them through circumstances that developed their trust in Him. When Joshua eventually led them

into the land of Canaan, they had to defeat the current occupants
of the land before they could occupy it. (The land called Canaan
in the Bible includes modern-day

> The easiest way is not
> always the best way.

Israel, the West Bank and Gaza,
Jordan, and the southern portion of
Syria and Lebanon.)

The Israelites had to be ready for war when they entered
Canaan. God used their trials in the wilderness to prepare them
for the battles and the work that lay ahead of them. Although only
two of the original group entered Canaan, others who were born
in the wilderness also entered. The total number who entered
Canaan is estimated to be 2,500,000. This included 601,730 men
(Numbers 26:51), plus women and children. Joshua led this multi-
tude to the town of Jericho, and they conquered it and went from
there as God led them. Just as the Israelites had to be ready for
war, we must be ready to stand firm against the attacks of the
devil.

Please take time to read this Scripture passage carefully and
think about what we can learn from it:

> Be well balanced (temperate, sober of mind), be vigilant
> and cautious at all times; for that enemy of yours, the
> devil, roams around like a lion roaring [in fierce hunger],
> seeking someone to seize upon and devour. Withstand
> him; be firm in faith [against his onset—rooted, estab-
> lished, strong, immovable, and determined], knowing
> that the same (identical) sufferings are appointed to your
> brotherhood (the whole body of Christians) throughout
> the world. And after you have suffered a little while, the
> God of all grace [Who imparts all blessing and favor], Who
> has called you to His [own] eternal glory in Christ Jesus,
> will Himself complete and make you what you ought to

be, establish and ground you securely, and strengthen, and settle you.

1 Peter 5:8–10 AMPC

Notice that this passage says we must be "rooted, established, strong, immovable, and determined" (v. 9). Do these words describe you? Remember, whatever you may be going through right now will pass. Your job is to wait on God with a good attitude and be obedient to do anything He asks you to do.

As you read this passage, you may wonder why God would allow us to suffer for a little while before He makes us what we ought to be (v. 10). I believe He lets us suffer in our trials for a period of time so that when He does deliver us, we will know for sure that He has done it. While we wait on Him in the midst of our suffering, we usually try everything we can think of until we run out of our own strength and lean entirely on Him.

There is a big difference between the works of our flesh and the works of God. Works of the flesh are rooted in our ideas of what we should do to solve our problems, and they rarely work because we have not involved God in them. He will not allow us to succeed without Him, because if He did, we would take the glory and credit for ourselves, become puffed up with pride, and become useless for the work He has for us to do.

God waits until we have exhausted all of our own works, and then He changes us. When we realize that He has done the work, we are thankful and give Him the glory. Remember that God told the Israelites He led them in the wilderness to humble them and to prove them to see if they would keep His commands or not (Deuteronomy 8:2–3). This humbling was necessary in order for them to become obedient to Him. I have heard

> God waits until you have exhausted your own works before He changes you.

that faith in God is not real faith until it is all you are holding on to. Trials purify us and test our motives, and they exercise and strengthen our faith. When we experience the good that comes from our trials, we can truly thank God for them, because we know they will ultimately make us better if we do not let them make us bitter.

> *Trials exercise and strengthen your faith.*

Rejoice always, pray continually, give thanks in all circumstances; for this is God's will for you in Christ Jesus.

1 Thessalonians 5:16–18

Emotional Hearers

I characterize the believers in Mark 4:16–17—those who got excited when they heard the Word but only stayed enthusiastic until trouble came—as "emotional hearers." When we allow our emotions to rule us, we will be defeated. The psalmist writes that we are blessed when God disciplines and instructs us, that we may learn to keep ourselves "calm in the days of adversity, until the [inevitable] pit of corruption is dug for the wicked" (Psalm 94:12–13 AMPC).

Are you able to stay calm when trouble comes your way or when you are suffering? I've made a lot of progress in this area of my life, but I certainly still have a long way to go. Not allowing myself to become upset requires me to control my emotions instead of letting them control me.

Unless we want to keep going around and around the same mountain, making the same mistakes over and over, we should become quick learners. I often say, "In God's school, we never flunk out; we just get to take the same tests over and over until we pass them." At one point, when the Israelites were in the wilderness, God told them that they had been at the same mountain long enough (Deuteronomy 1:6). If this describes you, it is time to move to the next level with God. It is time to get out of the wilderness and enjoy living in God's promises by trusting and relying on Him.

> You must take the same test over and over until you pass it.

God wants us to be led by His Holy Spirit, who lives in each person who believes in Jesus. He will always lead us to do what is wise, not just what feels good to our emotions. Emotions have been said to be the believer's number one enemy, and I believe this. The Israelites behaved emotionally anytime they encountered suffering or even discomfort. Maybe they were offended by their difficulties because they were God's chosen people. As such, they may have believed they should have been exempt from hardships.

Trouble stirs our emotions and prompts us to say things we should not say. When emotions are running high, we are wise to talk less in order to avoid saying anything that gives the devil opportunity to attack us.

> Trouble prompts you to say things you shouldn't.

When trouble comes your way, don't let it offend you. Trust God to help you get through it and to work something good out of it. This way, you can be blessed in the midst of your mess.

CHAPTER 7

Be Careful What You Say

Don't mix bad words with your bad mood. You will have many opportunities to change a mood, but you will never get the opportunity to replace the words you spoke.

Anonymous

When life gets messy, our moods tend to sink. When they do, we need to be careful about what we say. We may become grouchy with other people and hurt their feelings or even damage a relationship. We often say things we later wish we had not said, but then it is too late. Once words are spoken, they cannot be retrieved. All words contain some kind of power, whether negative or positive, uplifting or downgrading. We are wise to remember that our words have the power to either help or hurt us and other people. Proverbs 18:21 puts it this way: "Death and life are in the power of the tongue, and those who love it and indulge it will eat its fruit and bear the consequences of their words" (AMP).

> Your words have the power to either help people or hurt them.

If you already have problems in your life, why make them worse by speaking negatively? What kinds of words do you usually speak when trouble comes? I know the kinds of things I used to say before I learned better. I made statements such as "It never fails; we always have some kind of trouble messing up our lives," "This is more than I can take; I just give up," and "I'm sick and tired of having problems." If you are already having a problem, why declare that you are sick and tired on top of it? Be very careful about the words you speak, because according to Proverbs 13:3, "Those who guard their lips preserve their lives, but those who speak rashly will come to ruin."

We often speak out of our frustration without realizing that positive, faith-filled words have the power to help lift us out of a situation and change the way we feel in the midst of it. No wonder Jesus said He would not talk much after His suffering had begun (John 14:30). It is better to say nothing than to say the wrong thing. If you cannot say something that will help you or someone else, don't say anything at all.

Words have consequences, and they affect the outcome of our lives. If we struggle to speak life-giving words during times of trouble, we're better off being quiet. Speaking positive, life-giving words is helpful, but speaking words that are filled with negativity and death only makes a situation worse.

As I mentioned, when trouble comes, emotions run wild, and the first thing we want to do is talk about how we feel. What we should do instead is speak God's Word over the situation, making comments such as these:

- "This hurts me, but I believe God will work something good out of it."
- "This is hard, but God will give me the strength to deal with it."
- "I wish this wasn't happening, but it will come to an end."
- "I'm hurting, but God will comfort me and show me what to do."
- "This situation seems unfair, but I know God loves me and He will reward me if I keep doing His will."

When we are hurting, we don't have to pretend we are not struggling, but we are to fight the good fight of faith while we are hurting and do spiritual warfare with our words.

I didn't know anything about the power of words until I was in my late thirties, and what I have learned since then has been life-changing. I still work with God every day to help me speak words of life instead of words of death, because I am aware of the power of words. And little by little, I am making steady progress. Always look at your progress rather than at how far you still have to go, because this will encourage you to keep pressing on.

It is amazing how often we cause a problem by speaking careless words. Yesterday I spoke one sentence to someone, and that one sentence opened the door to a lengthy heated conversation that ended up upsetting me and costing me a good night's sleep. Oh, how I wish I had not said anything, but it's too late now. The damage has been done, and I cannot do anything about it. But I can let the situation be yet another lesson on the power of words, a lesson that will hopefully help me use more wisdom in the future as I choose what to say or not say to people.

Speak to the Mountain

God's Word teaches us that we can speak to our mountains (problems) and tell them to throw themselves into the sea:

> "Have faith in God," Jesus answered. "Truly I tell you, if anyone says to this mountain, 'Go, throw yourself into the sea,' and does not doubt in their heart but believes that what they say will happen, it will be done for them. Therefore I tell you, whatever you ask for in prayer, believe that you have received it, and it will be yours. And when you stand praying, if you hold anything against anyone, forgive them, so that your Father in heaven may forgive you your sins."
>
> Mark 11:22–26

Notice that this Scripture passage mentions speaking *to* a mountain (representing a problem), not *about* it (v. 23). Usually, when we have a problem, we typically talk about it to anyone who will listen, but what good does that do? Perhaps we do need to vent to someone, but God is a better sounding board than anyone else.

Talk to your problems instead of about them.

Try talking *to* your problems instead of talking *about* them. Remind them of what God's Word says. Here are some examples of good ways to speak to your problems:

- Problem, God is on my side, and He always gives me victory (2 Corinthians 2:14).
- No weapon formed against me shall prevail (Isaiah 54:17).
- I am more than a conqueror through Christ, who loves me (Romans 8:37).
- I will not fear; what can mere mortals do to me? (Hebrews 13:6).
- My God will meet all my needs (Philippians 4:19).
- I can do all things through Christ, who is my strength (Philippians 4:13).
- My enemies may come against me one way, but they will flee before me seven ways (Deuteronomy 28:7).
- I submit myself to God; I resist the devil, and he has to flee (James 4:7).

When you think and speak what the Bible says, you are declaring God's Word. Jesus declared God's Word when the devil tempted Him in the wilderness (Matthew 4:4, 7, 10), and just as He defeated the enemy, you will too.

As you speak positive words filled with faith, you will be strengthened and encouraged. It will help you believe that your problems are not bigger than God and that with Him on your side, you can handle anything.

Speak God's Word to your troubles, pray, and believe that what you have asked for will be yours. Before asking God for anything, be sure you have no unforgiveness in your heart against anyone (Mark 11:25). The only thing left to do is believe God is working and that your breakthrough will come soon. In the meantime, you can enjoy your life.

God promises we will get what we ask for if it is within His will, but He doesn't tell us exactly when we will get it.

> Now this is the confidence that we have in Him, that if we ask anything according to His will, He hears us. And if we know that He hears us, whatever we ask, we know that we have the petitions that we have asked of Him.
>
> 1 John 5:14–15 NKJV

There will probably be some waiting involved, and during that time it is important to be careful about what we say and to stay happy, because the joy of the Lord is our strength (Nehemiah 8:10).

I have taught many messages on the power of our words and written two books on the subject, *Change Your Words, Change Your Life* and *Power Words*, but I never tire of mentioning it again. Speaking what God says always helps me, and it will help you too if you keep at it.

Who Is Religious?

The Bible tells us that truly religious people must bridle (discipline) their tongue. "If anyone thinks he is religious and does not bridle his tongue but deceives his heart, this person's religion is worthless" (James 1:26 ESV). I regret saying this, but some of the meanest people I have ever met were people who considered themselves "religious." They performed the external duties of religion (church attendance, Bible reading, giving offerings, and so on), but they wouldn't lift a finger to help anyone and were the first to criticize and judge anyone who didn't fit into their particular brand of religion.

In Matthew 23, Jesus had scathing words for people who practiced this kind of religion. The most religious people of His day were called Pharisees. They studied the Torah (Old Testament Law) and carefully followed all the religious rules and regulations of their day. Sadly, they were also very critical of anyone who wasn't like they were, and they were hypocrites. They told others what to do but did not do it themselves. Jesus said they were "like whitewashed tombs," full of dead people's bones (v. 27). They did their good works so other people would see them. They put heavy burdens of rules and regulations on people but wouldn't lift a finger to help them. I have met many pharisee-type people in my life, and I have seen firsthand that most of them don't bridle their tongue.

Jesus sets us free from the rigorous regulations of the law and opens the way for us to have relationship with God the Father through faith in Him. God's moral code is no longer on stone tablets (the Ten Commandments), but He has put His law in our minds and written it on our hearts (Hebrews 8:10). If we learn to follow what God puts in our hearts instead of our emotions, we will speak more words of life.

God's desire is for us to enjoy life (John 10:10). First Peter 3:10 says: "Whoever would love life and see good days must keep their tongue from evil and their lips from deceitful speech." We can see from this scripture that our words not only affect other people, but they also affect us. Evil words also grieve the Holy Spirit, and that is something we should be diligent to avoid.

> *Evil words grieve the Holy Spirit.*

Do not let any unwholesome talk come out of your mouths,
but only what is helpful for building others up according

to their needs, that it may benefit those who listen. And do not grieve the Holy Spirit of God, with whom you were sealed for the day of redemption.

Ephesians 4:29–30

Goodness and Mercy Follow Us

King David had many enemies. But in Psalm 23, he writes to the Lord, "I will fear no evil, for you are with me" (v. 4). Even in the midst of his battles, he experienced God's blessings. He also writes, "You prepare a table before me in the presence of my enemies. You anoint my head with oil; my cup overflows" (v. 5). When he says, "My cup overflows," he means that he has more than enough to meet his needs. This psalm ends with David declaring, "Surely your goodness and love will follow me all the days of my life" (v. 6). We tend to

You can see God do good things for you while your enemies watch.

think we cannot enjoy life as long as we have problems, but this is not true. Like David, we can see God do good things for us while our enemies watch. Even in the midst of his troubles, he was blessed, and we should expect to be blessed in the midst of our difficulties too.

We serve a God who calls things that don't exist yet as if they already exist (Romans 4:17 AMPC), and we can do the same. Just as David did, even during difficulties we can call ourselves blessed, and in the midst of lack we can declare that we have more than enough. Remember that Jesus promised that we can have peace amid trouble (John 16:33). We can be blessed in our mess.

David spoke positive, uplifting words while experiencing negative circumstances, and we should follow his example. The words we speak during times of trouble are vitally important. Throughout the Psalms, we see the psalmist talking openly to God about his troubles, but he always ends by declaring his trust for God and his expectation of being blessed. In Psalm 13:2–5 (AMPC) David writes:

> How long must I lay up cares within me and have sorrow in my heart day after day? How long shall my enemy exalt himself over me? Consider and answer me, O Lord my God; lighten the eyes [of my faith to behold Your face in the pitchlike darkness], lest I sleep the sleep of death, lest my enemy say, I have prevailed over him, and those that trouble me rejoice when I am shaken. But I have trusted, leaned on, and been confident in Your mercy and loving-kindness; my heart shall rejoice and be in high spirits in Your salvation.

Declaring that we will be blessed as we go through trials and tribulations doesn't make sense to the natural (unspiritual) person, but we are spiritual people who look beyond our circumstances and walk by faith. We should walk by faith and talk by faith.

I recommend that you speak blessings over yourself and your loved ones each day. Not because you have been good and deserve blessings, but because God is good, and He has promised to bless us.

Ask for God's Help

James 3:8 tells us that "no human being can tame the tongue. It is a restless evil, full of deadly poison." The apostle James also writes of how a small spark starts a forest fire, and we learn from this example that just a few wrong words can cause big trouble in our life (James 3:5). Many times, I have wished I could take back words I'd spoken that created problems in my relationship with someone. We cannot tame the tongue by willpower alone, but we can ask for God's help and learn to think before we speak. Based on Psalm 141:3, I pray daily, "God, put a guard over my mouth, so I won't sin against You with my words."

Controlling the tongue may be one of our biggest challenges, and it is one we need to pray about again and again. Remember, "Death and life are in the power of the tongue, and they who indulge in it shall eat the fruit of it [for death or life]" (Proverbs 18:21 AMPC).

Do you know that you can improve your own health by speaking kind words? Proverbs 16:24 says, "Kind words are like honey—sweet to the soul and healthy for the body" (NLT), and Proverbs 12:18 says, "The tongue of the wise brings healing."

I encourage you to take one week and listen to the words people speak. If you do, it won't take long to understand why they have problems in life. We can give ourselves that same test and gain insight into our difficulties. Let's make a commitment to be more careful about what we say at all times, especially when we have problems that stir up our emotions.

How Jesus Handled His Temptation

There is no better example for us than Jesus, so let's see how He handled a particular difficulty presented in the form of a great temptation. Matthew 4:1–2 tells us that Jesus was led by the Holy Spirit "into the wilderness to be tempted by the devil. After fasting forty days and forty nights, he was hungry," and I am sure He was tired. Times when we are hungry, sick, and/or tired are times when the devil loves to attack us, because we are more vulnerable than we are when we feel strong.

In the wilderness, the devil tried to get Jesus to do things that did not agree with God's Word. He knew Jesus was hungry and tested Him, saying, "If you are the Son of God, tell these stones to become bread" (Matthew 4:3). That would have been easy for Jesus to do, but He talked back to the devil, saying, "It is written: 'Man shall not live on bread alone, but on every word that comes from the mouth of God'" (Matthew 4:4). Jesus knew He could do without bread, but He could not do without His relationship with His Father. He knew—and always chose—what was the most important. Jesus knew the Word and spoke the Word.

Next, according to Matthew 4:5–6:

> Then the devil took him to the holy city and had him stand on the highest point of the temple. "If you are the Son of God," he said, "throw yourself down. For it is written: 'He will command his angels concerning you, and they will lift you up in their hands, so that you will not strike your foot against a stone.'"

Satan knows Scripture, and he will try to twist it to draw us away from the freeing power of its truth. Jesus immediately answered him, "It is also written: 'Do not put the Lord your God to the test'" (Matthew 4:7).

In both these temptations, Satan was trying to get Jesus to prove He was the Son of God. But Jesus knew who He was and had no need to prove it. When we know who we are in Christ, we should not feel we need to prove ourselves to other people. We are never truly free until we have no need to impress anyone.

When you know who you are in Christ, you don't need to prove yourself to others.

In the third and final temptation, the devil took Jesus to a high mountain and showed Him all the splendor of all the kingdoms of the world. "'All this I will give you,' he said, 'if you will bow down and worship me'" (Matthew 4:9). Jesus responded, "Away from me, Satan! For it is written: 'Worship the Lord your God, and serve him only'" (Matthew 4:10).

This is perhaps the temptation we fail to resist most frequently. Satan tempts us to compromise in order to have something the world offers us, and we fail to realize that if we will simply wait on God, He will give us something much better than anything the world could possibly offer.

After Jesus stood strong against these temptations, "the devil left him, and angels came and attended him" (Matthew 4:11). Jesus passed His tests, and angels came to comfort, refresh, and strengthen Him. I don't know about you, but I could use a few visits from an angel!

I don't think we have any idea how often the devil tempts us with lies, trying to deceive us. Many people in the world don't even know he exists or that he is their real problem. He lies, and they believe his lies and are therefore deceived. I was one of those people for a long, long time. Although I recognize many of the enemy's lies now, I know there are times when, through a lack of diligence on my part, I fail to recognize them. There are other times when I am not aggressive enough in resisting him right away, as Jesus did. Although we shouldn't, sometimes we become lazy in resisting the devil. When we do, he takes advantage of it.

After Satan tempted Jesus in the wilderness, the Amplified Bible says that "he [temporarily] left Him until a more opportune time" (Luke 4:13 AMP). I think it is safe to say that the devil will never completely leave us alone. He will always look for opportunities to make us miserable or hold us in bondage. So we always need to be alert and on our guard.

Immediately after Jesus passed the tests in the wilderness, He began His public ministry and worked many miracles. We see again that after the testing came the blessing. Why would Jesus need to be tested and tempted? Surely, His Father knew He would pass. It was important for Jesus as the Son of Man to pass Satan's tests in His humanity, because Hebrews 4:15 teaches us that He was tempted in all ways, just as we are, yet He never sinned. This is why He can have empathy and understanding toward us when we face similar trials.

Jesus knew the importance of words, and when He was under pressure from the devil, He always made sure to resist speaking from His emotions. He chose His words carefully, and so should we.

CHAPTER 8

Understand the Power of a Good Attitude

Your attitude, not your aptitude, will determine your altitude.

Zig Ziglar[10]

You have probably heard the phrase "Your attitude determines your altitude," and it is true. An attitude is a settled way of thinking or feeling about something, and it is reflected in our behavior. We might say that our attitude is our thought life turned inside out. A good attitude has the power to change a negative circumstance into a blessing. If our attitude is up, we can expect to have an above average life and if our attitude is down, we will have a below average life. John Maxwell says, "You are only an attitude away from success."[11]

A good attitude makes up for a lack of aptitude. I would rather work with someone who is positive and easy to get along with but perhaps not as skilled as someone who is highly skilled and has a bad attitude.

> A good attitude makes up for a lack of aptitude.

Philippians 2:5 talks about Jesus' attitude: "Let this same attitude and purpose and [humble] mind be in you which was in Christ Jesus: [Let Him be your example in humility]" (AMPC).

Later in the same chapter, in verse 8, we read that Jesus humbled Himself and became obedient to death on the cross. Verse 9 continues: "Therefore God exalted him to the highest place and gave him the name that is above every name." Jesus was willing to take the lowest place, and God gave Him the highest place. A good attitude brings reward and blessing.

Earlier in the book, I wrote about people who are offended when they have trouble. This reflects a bad attitude. However, people who are humble never assume they are too good to have to deal with a problem, and when they do have a mess in their lives, they will likely be thankful that it isn't worse than it is.

A humble attitude affects many areas of our lives in a positive way. People with a humble attitude never think more highly of themselves than they should. They don't see other people as beneath them, and they don't mistreat the people over whom they have authority simply because they know they can. They are willing to do jobs others might consider lowly, they usually have a servant's attitude, and they are generally pleasant people.

No situation in life brings out our true attitudes like trials and troubles do. Difficult situations are called trials because they *try* us, and through them, we find out what we are truly made of. The way we handle challenges and hardships reveals how strong we are spiritually. It shows us how patient and thankful we are, and it teaches us many other lessons about ourselves. It is easy to think we are full of faith until our faith is tested. Then we discover just how much faith we really have.

Going through the tests God allows in our lives is good for us because it helps us truly know ourselves. These experiences bring out our weaknesses and flaws, which allows us to work with God toward changing them for the better. Tests also bring out our strengths and make us even stronger in those areas.

Trials develop patience and perseverance, according to various translations of James 1:3 (NKJV, NIV). But as I have been through trials in my life, I've found they brought a lot of other things out of me long before I got to patience. Mostly they brought out bad attitudes that needed to be changed before God could use me. Imma-

> *Trials develop patience and perseverance.*

ture Christians' first response to trouble is usually to feel sorry for themselves and to think and speak negatively. However, we can grow past such bad attitudes and actually have good attitudes during trouble if we believe the difficulty will ultimately produce blessings in our life.

Take an Attitude Inventory

I encourage you to take time to truly think about your attitude and especially consider how you react when you go through difficulties. Do you get discouraged or depressed when trouble comes, or do you remind yourself that everyone goes through painful situations and that your hardship won't last forever? Do you stay positive, or do you let negativity take over and cause you to have a sour view toward life? Do you maintain a thankful attitude in all circumstances, as God's Word teaches us to do (1 Thessalonians 5:18)? Being thankful for what you do have instead of being upset about what you don't have is powerful, and it is pleasing to God. I think it is good for us to ask ourselves questions like the ones in this paragraph. It is very important to truly know ourselves.

If our attitude begins to sink when trouble comes, we can remind ourselves of how important it is to keep a positive outlook. We can always change an attitude that is headed in the wrong direction before it gets too bad. Keeping a good attitude requires self-control.

> Keeping a good attitude requires self-control.

God convicts us of problem areas in our lives. He doesn't do this so we can feel guilty and bad about ourselves, but so we can work with Him to change them. We cannot do anything about something unless we are aware of it. Be thankful if God shows you that you have a bad attitude about something. Repent and ask Him to help you change it.

When we encounter trouble, we have two options: We can be upset about the problem, or we can think about how much worse it could be. I recently took a fall and landed on one side of my face, my knees, my elbow, and my ribs. Dave was in the room when I fell, and it frightened him because he thought I would be really hurt, based on how hard I fell. I could have broken some teeth or seriously damaged other parts of my body, but all I had was a very sore elbow and a couple of bruises. Dave and I have talked many times about how God must have had angels protecting me or I would have done some serious damage to myself.

No matter how bad a situation is, it could be worse, and there are people who have much worse situations than we do. When I cannot sleep at night, I can at least thank God that I have a bed to lie in and that I'm not homeless. When I am stuck in traffic, I can thank God that I have a car and don't have to walk to where I want to go.

When you have a bad day at work, think of the person who has been out of work for three months. Should you find yourself the victim of someone's bitterness, judgment, or criticism, remember that things could be worse. You could be that bitter, unhappy, critical person!

> *There are worse things than being a victim of someone else's bitterness.*

Misery Is an Option

When we find ourselves miserable, we should realize that misery is an option and that we can change our mood by changing our thoughts and attitudes. Misery makes bad company, and if I am going to be by myself in a situation, I would rather be there with a happy attitude than a miserable one.

> *Regular attitude adjustments are needed in life.*

Ephesians 4:23 says we are to be made new in the attitude of our minds, and the amplification of this verse says, "having a fresh mental and spiritual attitude" (AMPC). Regular attitude adjustments are needed in life. In fact, our attitude needs constant attention to keep it going in the right direction. Some people must work harder than others to keep a good attitude simply because of their temperament. Some people seem to be born upbeat and positive, and they are that way most of the time without having to make much effort. However, there are those of us who, either due to temperament or to life experiences, tend to be a bit more down and negative. It is easy for us to quickly see what is wrong in almost every situation. I say "we" because I am in this group, and I admit that I have had to work at choosing to stay positive in negative situations.

I am thankful for all the progress I have made in keeping a good attitude, by the grace of God. I would say I am now a more positive person than a negative one, but there are still days I have to discipline myself in order to keep the attitude I know God wants me to have. If you are this way too, you don't have to feel bad about it, because we all have weak areas. The important thing is that we recognize them and work with God to keep improving.

How to Be Happy

I believe everyone just wants to be happy. In the world, happiness is based on what is happening, but in God's kingdom, we do not have to live that way. First Peter 3:14 says, "But even in case you should suffer for the sake of righteousness, [you are] blessed (happy, to be envied). Do not dread or be afraid of their threats, nor be disturbed [by their opposition]" (AMPC). Why? Because if we suffer in order to do what is right, we will be blessed in the end. The way to avoid misery in the midst of trials is to keep it in perspective, meaning to choose to not view it as bigger or more consequential than it is and to see it in the context of everything else—especially the good things—in your life. To keep a proper perspective on suffering, remember that God is good and look beyond what is happening right now to the end result. Also, we need to believe that God works all things for good for those who love Him and are "called according to His plan and purpose" (Romans 8:28 AMP) and that what Satan means for harm, God intends for good (Genesis 50:20). This is really exciting when you think about it. When the enemy throws trouble at us, all he is really doing is putting us in a position to be blessed if we keep a good attitude during the difficulty.

> The best way to avoid misery is to keep it in perspective.

The third part of this book is devoted to an in-depth look at the Beatitudes, which are found in Matthew 5:3–12 as part of Jesus' Sermon on the Mount (Matthew 5–7). But for now I would like to focus on just one, found in Matthew 5:11–12: "Blessed are you when people insult you, persecute you and falsely say all kinds of evil against you because of me. Rejoice and be glad, because great is your reward in heaven." God rewards right choices.

The world says we can be happy only if we take care of ourselves and live self-serving lives, but Jesus says we can be happy if we serve others (Acts 20:35). He washed His disciples' feet as an example of servanthood and spoke to them about the importance of

> You can be happy if you serve others.

serving others (John 13:1–15). Afterward, He said, "If you know these things, you are blessed [happy and favored by God] if you put them into practice [and faithfully do them]" (John 13:17 AMP).

One of the best times to get your mind off of yourself and focus on what you can do for someone else is when you are hurting and experiencing trials and trouble. Having a good attitude in the midst of difficulty confuses the devil. He expects pain and trouble to upset us and make us miserable, and when it doesn't, he loses and we win.

If we are miserable, it shows on our faces. One of the most important things we wear is our facial expression. The Bible refers to this as our "countenance." For example, Cain looked sad and depressed because he was jealous of Abel (Genesis 4:5–6 AMPC).

If we are jealous of other people, wishing we had their lives instead of enjoying our own, we will have a bad attitude that will make us miserable. But if we embrace our life, even with its imperfections, and we don't complain but are thankful instead, we will have a good life.

Our attitude is the prophet of our future. It is our best friend or our worst enemy; it is what draws people to us or repels them. It is the primary force that determines whether we succeed or fail. Robert J. Hastings said, "Places and circumstances never guarantee happiness. You must decide within yourself whether you want to be happy."[12]

> Your attitude is the prophet of your future.

How to Maintain a Good Attitude

Here are some lessons I have learned about maintaining a good attitude. I remind myself of them from time to time and find them helpful. I hope they will be helpful to you too.

1. Maintain the right attitude when you find yourself in a mess. Everybody can have a good attitude when things go their way.

- As soon as you sense your attitude losing altitude, make an adjustment.

- Remember that maintaining the right attitude is easier than regaining the right attitude.
- Resist the devil at his onset, meaning from the beginning of his attempt to discourage you or bring negativity to your mind, when you first sense he is trying to upset you, harass you, or discourage you. "Be well balanced (temperate, sober of mind), be vigilant and cautious at all times; for that enemy of yours, the devil, roams around like a lion roaring [in fierce hunger], seeking someone to seize upon and devour" (1 Peter 5:8 AMPC).
- Don't pray for a life without trials or trouble. Jesus says we *will* face difficulty (John 16:33). Instead, pray that you will keep a good attitude when you do encounter hardships.
- John Maxwell says, "Circumstances don't make you what you are, they reveal what you are!"[13]

2. Realize that the difficulty won't last forever.

- Robert Schuller said, "The good news is that the bad news can be turned into good news when you change your attitude."[14]
- You will survive. Just think of all the other situations you have made it through in victory and know that the one you are currently facing will be no different.

3. Don't make major decisions during your time of trouble if you don't have to.

- I have said many times, "Let emotions subside before you decide."
- You cannot always avoid making decisions until your trouble passes. If you do have to make a big decision, try your best not to base your decision on your emotions.

4. Seek God's presence at all times. Stay close to Him. He will comfort you and guide you.

- James 4:8 says, "Draw near to God and He will draw near to you" (NKJV).
- Proverbs 3:5–6 says, "Trust in the Lord with all your heart and lean not on your own understanding; in all your ways submit to him, and he will make your paths straight."

5. Try to keep your situation in perspective. The way you view your circumstances will determine how you think and feel about them.

- Look at everything that is good and right in your life, not just at the one situation that is negative.
- Corrie Ten Boom said, "Child, you have to learn to see things in the right proportions. Learn to see great things great and small things small."[15]

Great things can happen during seasons of major hardship. Books written by Jeanne Guyon have profoundly affected me and thousands of others. She was imprisoned in France from 1695–1703 and did much writing during this time. Sir Walter Raleigh wrote *The History of the World* during a thirteen-year imprisonment in the Tower of London (1603–1616). Martin Luther translated the New Testament from Greek to German while confined for his own safety in the Wartburg Castle in 1521–1522. Ludwig van Beethoven wrote his Ninth Symphony, which includes "Ode to Joy," in 1824 while almost totally deaf and after enduring great hardship throughout his life.

> *True greatness always emerges during times of crisis.*

If a person is truly great, their true greatness always emerges during times of crisis.

Here is the story of Katie Piper, who has suffered greatly and decided to have a good attitude during extremely difficult circumstances.

Acid Attack Survivor Katie Piper Is Moving On and Helping Others

Katie Piper thought her life was over when a hired hitman threw sulphuric acid in her face. The brutal assault left the 24-year-old up and coming model/TV personality disfigured and fighting for her life. But she's come a long way over the years. And now, 33-year-old acid attack survivor Katie Piper is using her story to help inspire others!

The Attack

Katie dated Daniel Lynch—the man who orchestrated the attack that forever changed her life—for just two weeks. Daniel turned violent after the brief romance ended. In a fit of jealousy, he hired a hitman named Stefan. Stefan approached Katie on the streets of London, dousing her in sulphuric acid....

The Aftermath

The corrosive acid severely burned Katie's nose, throat and mouth, as well as partially blinded her in one eye. It terribly disfigured her face, almost as though it had melted. The short time it took Stefan to toss the acid, a matter of mere seconds, completely changed the trajectory of Katie's life....

The recovery process ahead was long and painful....

Overcoming

Over roughly the next decade, Katie endured hundreds of surgeries. She's worn special masks, had tubes in her nose and tons of other treatments. But with the love and support of her friends and family, she persevered.

"In the beginning the surgery overtook my life," says Katie. "Now I have a life and my surgery fits around it."

Katie's progress has been miraculous. God has transformed the horrific and traumatic event into a platform for Katie. And it's one she is incredibly passionate about.

Katie began speaking publicly about her experience as an acid attack survivor, developing a heart for women who've become obsessed with self-image. Katie has made it her mission to inspire and encourage women to accept themselves as they are. She even started her own charity, the Katie Piper Foundation, to support other burn victims.

Moving On

Katie's perseverance has been an inspiration to so many over the years.

The acid attack survivor has found happiness in her personal life, too. After such a malicious attack, it had to be difficult to trust again. But God led Katie to Richard Sutton, and the two wed in 2015....

God blessed the couple with a beautiful daughter, Belle. And Katie's past has made her even more appreciative of the gifts God gives us in life.

"The whole chapter of getting married and having a baby was something I had hoped for—but I knew it was a luxury and it doesn't happen to everybody," Katie said. "I felt even more joyful because I wasn't sure if it was something I'd be privileged enough to experience."

What she's endured has been incredibly difficult. But God clearly had a big purpose for Katie's life!

"And we know that all things work together for good to them that love God, to them who are the called according to his purpose" (Romans 8:28 [KJV]).[16]

Nothing does more harm to the devil's plans for our destruction and misery than maintaining a good attitude amid a bad situation.

Always maintain a good attitude in the midst of a bad situation.

CHAPTER 9

Stay Positive

Nothing is so sour that it can't be sweetened by a good attitude.

Woodrow Kroll[17]

To see the power and effect of a positive attitude compared to a negative one, we can look at the Israelites and their journey through difficult times in the wilderness as they moved toward the Promised Land. The journey had its challenges, I'm sure, but I also believe the Israelites made it much worse because they did not think positively about it. Negative thinking limits God because He works through our faith, and there is nothing negative about faith. Negative thinking also limits our potential. As long as we have a negative attitude, we are not creative or energetic. We have little desire to do anything except complain.

> You cannot be creative or energetic with a negative attitude.

While the Israelites were in the wilderness, God sent twelve spies into the Promised Land so they could see that it was indeed plentiful, as He had said (Numbers 13:2–20). When the spies returned, ten of them gave a negative report about the land, and two, Joshua and Caleb, gave a positive report. All twelve spies saw an abundance of good fruit in the land, but they also saw the giants who lived there. The ten focused more on the giants than on the fruit and felt they could not defeat them. Joshua and Caleb also saw the giants, but they believed they could conquer them (Numbers 13:27–33; 14:6–9). Joshua and Caleb ended up being the only two men of their generation who entered the Promised Land (Numbers 14:30–34; 32:11–13).

The ten spies made an insightful comment about themselves and the giants when they said: "We seemed like grasshoppers in our own eyes, and we looked the same to them" (Numbers 13:33). It is interesting that the way we see ourselves affects how other people see us also. If we are confident, people will have confidence in us, and if we are not, they won't.

The Israelites were weary from their time in the wilderness, and they needed some good news, but when the ten spies came out with such a negative report, all the Israelites wept all night (Numbers 14:1).

> Being positive means seeing hope in the midst of your problems.

Being positive does not mean we deny the existence of our problems; it simply means we see hope in the midst of them. We believe God can and will help us, and we look forward to something good happening.

David writes, "[What, what would have become of me] had I not believed that I would see the Lord's goodness in the land of the living! Wait and hope for and expect the Lord; be brave and of good courage and let your heart be stout and enduring. Yes, wait for and hope for and expect the Lord" (Psalm 27:13–14 AMPC).

> Expect something good to happen in your life.

Expect something good to happen in your life. Your happy thoughts will energize you to get through the difficulty you are enduring. When we are having problems, our thoughts and attitudes immediately start to sink and become negative and sad, but we can interrupt their downfall by choosing to think positive thoughts and speak positive words. Positive people are much happier than negative ones.

The Israelites never really saw beyond their circumstances. Their attitude throughout their entire journey was negative. Notice some of the comments they made when problems arose:

All the Israelites grumbled against Moses and Aaron, and the whole assembly said to them, "If only we had died in

Egypt! Or in this wilderness! Why is the Lord bringing us
to this land only to let us fall by the sword? Our wives and
children will be taken as plunder. Wouldn't it be better for
us to go back to Egypt?" And they said to each other, "We
should choose a leader and go back to Egypt."

Numbers 14:2–4

I certainly would not have wanted to travel with this bunch of
people. They could drag anyone into a pit of despair. They did not
see what was possible with God on their side; they saw only what
had been and what was. Their thoughts, words, and attitudes were
negative and hopeless.

You Can Have All You See

Those who look at the world with the eye of faith see a future.
Abram and his nephew Lot had parted due to strife among their
herdsmen. To restore peace, Abram gave most of his good land to
Lot (Genesis 13:5–11). Abram appeared to have lost much, but he
was actually about to get more. God told him, "Look around from
where you are, to the north and south, to the east and west. All
the land that you see I will give to you and your offspring forever"
(Genesis 13:14–15).

If you are experiencing trials and trouble right now, let me
encourage you to put this book aside for a few moments, close
your eyes, and see yourself with a future that is not full of problems. See the victory; see the change. Paul writes that God is able
to "do superabundantly, far over and above all that we [dare] ask
or think [infinitely beyond our highest prayers, desires, thoughts,
hopes, or dreams]" (Ephesians 3:20 AMPC). See with the eye of
faith and you will be amazed at what God does in your life.

Our enemy, the devil, tries to get you to have a negative attitude. But if you want to be blessed in your mess, choose to be positive even if you don't have one circumstance that seems to actually be positive. Have enough faith to see something good beyond your problems, and don't let someone else's negativity persuade you to give up your hopes and dreams.

When God called me into ministry, I knew a lot of people. Of all of them, only two gave me any encouragement. The rest of them said I couldn't be in ministry because I didn't have the right education. Even if I could do it, they said, I shouldn't do it because I am a woman, and one even said I didn't have the right personality. I am forever grateful that God gave me the grace and faith to trust Him more than I trusted the negative people in my life, because forty-five years later I am still in ministry.

The Power of a Positive Mind

Sometimes, before I speak publicly, I look at the faces of the people in the audience. I love to see the bright smiles and expressions of anticipation. But I typically also see a few who look downtrodden and discouraged. I don't know anything about these people, but their faces look sad. They appear as though they've lost hope and expect nothing positive to happen. Too often, people who have only negative expectations get exactly what they expect. I understand people who feel discouraged, because I was once one of them. I know they are engulfed in their problems and refuse to see beyond them.

> Positive minds produce positive lives.

I've learned that positive minds produce positive lives, but negative minds produce negative lives.

Matthew 8:5–10 tells the story of a Roman soldier whose servant was sick, and the soldier wanted Jesus to heal him. This wasn't uncommon—many people wanted Jesus to heal them or their loved ones in those days. But this soldier, instead of asking Jesus to come to his servant, expressed his belief that if Jesus would speak a word of healing, his servant would be healed (Matthew 8:8 NIV). Jesus marveled at his faith and sent His word to heal the servant. The soldier's positive mindset—his faith—led to positive results. He expected healing for his servant, and that's what he received.

Too often, we ask Jesus to heal us, provide for us financially, deliver us from problems, or help us in some other way, but we don't fully expect Him to bless us in the ways we have requested. We allow our minds to stay focused on our problems instead of believing God will bring the solutions we need. Doubt and unbelief will steal our faith if we aren't careful to keep our thoughts filled with faith and confidence in God.

Many years ago, I was extremely negative. I used to say that if I had two positive thoughts in a row, my mind would cramp. This is an exaggeration, of course, but it reflects the way I viewed myself. I believed, as many people do, that if I didn't expect anything good to happen, I wouldn't be disappointed when it didn't. What an unhappy way to live.

I could have excused my negative attitude by telling people about the many disappointments I had experienced. But my disappointment wasn't totally due to my lack of expectation. Some of it was rooted in the fact that I thought negatively and spoke negatively. When people told me about their spiritual victories, I thought, *That won't last.* When people spoke of their faith, I smiled, but I thought, *They are so naïve.* I thought often about how plans would go wrong or how people would disappoint me. I had experienced so many difficulties and disappointments in my life that I was afraid to expect anything good because I didn't want another disappointment.

Of course, I was not happy. Negative thinkers are never happy. Learning how negative thinking leads to an unhappy life was a long process for me, but once I realized what a negative person I was, I cried out to God to help me. I soon learned that if I kept studying God's Word, I could resist negative thoughts instead of letting them run my life. My responsibility was to become the kind of believer who honors God in my thoughts, words, and deeds.

Negative thinkers are never happy.

I understood the remorse David must have felt when he wrote Psalm 51. He starts with "Have mercy upon me, O God, according to Your steadfast love" (Psalm 51:1 AMPC). I especially meditated on verse 9: "Hide Your face from my sins and blot out all my guilt and iniquities" (AMPC). I hadn't sinned in the same way David did, but my negative thinking and bad attitude were still sin—not mere weaknesses or bad habits.

God's Word doesn't teach us to think negative thoughts but to think about things that are true, noble, admirable, and excellent (Philippians 4:8). As I continued studying Scripture and asking Him for help, He had mercy on me. He continues to free me from strongholds that Satan has built in my mind through negative thinking, and He's ready and waiting to do the same for you. Negative thoughts and people are all around us, because the devil knows that if we have faith in God and think positively about our future, good things will happen to us, and he will do all he can to prevent that from happening.

No Regrets

When we have regrets, we feel sad or disappointed about something that has happened or something we have done. Everyone

makes mistakes, sins, and experiences losses. But if we allow ourselves to wallow in regret too long, it steals the enjoyment of life

Never allow yourself to wallow in regret.

that God wants us to have, the joy
that Jesus died for us to have. He
said:

> The thief comes only in order to steal and kill and destroy.
> I came that they may have and enjoy life, and have it in
> abundance (to the full, till it overflows).
>
> John 10:10 AMPC

I spent many years not enjoying my life, but when I realized that
enjoying my life was God's will and that Jesus desires for me to have
a joy-filled life, I became determined to learn how to enjoy it. I grew
up in a home without enjoyment. It was actually a home filled with
fear and misery, and I simply never learned how to enjoy life or even
to think enjoying it was an option. There were many steps in my
learning how to enjoy life. For one, I had to learn that work was not
the only thing that gave me worth and value. I also had to learn how
to live without guilt. And I had to learn to live without regrets.

Of course, if I hurt someone or commit sin, I regret what I have
done. But I have also learned how to repent, ask for forgiveness,
receive it, and move on. God has taught me the uselessness of
guilt. Jesus has already completely and fully paid for our sins (1
Peter 2:24–25), and adding our guilt to it doesn't help anything.
Every fruit of guilt is negative. It makes us feel separated from
God, it negatively affects our prayer life, and it can make us hard
to get along with. We feel so bad about ourselves that we take out
our negativity on other people. Guilty feelings can even make us
sick. We may "feel" guilty, but God's Word says that once we have
repented, God forgives the sin and removes the guilt (Hebrews

9:14). I encourage you not to live by how you feel but to live by God's Word. Think about these words from Psalm 32:5 (AMPC):

> I acknowledged my sin to You, and my iniquity I did not hide. I said, I will confess my transgressions to the Lord [continually unfolding the past till all is told]—then You [instantly] forgave me the guilt and iniquity of my sin. Selah [pause, and calmly think of that]!

Because Jesus paid for our sins, when we repent, God forgives us and forgets our sin (Hebrews 8:12). If God has forgotten our sins, why should we keep remembering them and feeling regret over them? We may feel grief about our sins, but we are not supposed to live with that grief. Second Corinthians 7:10 says, "Godly sorrow brings repentance that leads to salvation and leaves no regret, but worldly sorrow brings death." Have godly sorrow for your sins—not worldly sorrow. Then repent, receive forgiveness, and move on. Remember, when we confess our sins to our faithful and just God, He will forgive us and purify us from all unrighteousness (1 John 1:8–9).

You may feel grief about your sins, but you are not supposed to live with it.

Part of living with positivity is learning how to let go of regrets instead of letting them pile up until your life is filled with them.

Yesterday I was grouchy with someone who is very kind to me and did not deserve my bad attitude at all. I apologized, and I repented. In order to turn what I did into something positive, I decided that

Look for an upside to your mistakes.

even though I should not have done it, at least I learned a lesson and gained experience that will help me not to do it again.

There is an upside to most of our mistakes, and we will find it if we look for it. If nothing else, at least we learn not to do the same thing again. We are so accustomed to being miserable each time we do something wrong that it may never occur to us that doing something wrong can be a positive development if we will look for the good that may come of it.

Dave and I have had confrontations that have made me miserable, but afterward our relationship was always better. Confrontation isn't fun, but anything we refuse to confront keeps chasing us. We cannot outrun our problems, because no matter how far we run, they will still be there when we stop.

> You cannot outrun your problems.

Dr. Norman Vincent Peale wrote a book called *The Power of Positive Thinking*. It was published in 1952 and is still in print today. It has sold millions of copies worldwide. Based on the success of this book, it seems obvious that people are interested in being more positive. We should all seek to be more positive. One way we can be blessed in our mess is to be positive even when negative things happen.

CHAPTER 10

Remain Patient

What then are we to do about our problems? We must learn to live with them until such time as God delivers us from them. If we cannot remove them, then we must pray for grace to endure them without murmuring. Problems patiently endured will work for our spiritual perfecting. They harm us only when we resist them or endure them unwillingly.

A. W. Tozer[18]

Patience is not simply the ability to wait; it includes our attitude and behavior while we wait. Waiting in life is not an option. Everyone waits. We wait on people to do the things we need them to do. We wait in the grocery store line. We wait at the doctor's office. When we're sick, we wait to get well. We wait in traffic. And we wait for God to deliver us from life's trials and tests.

Many years ago, I read that patience is a fruit of the Spirit that only grows under trial, and I have never forgotten it. Ouch! I wish I could get patience some other way, and you probably do too.

In the Amplified Bible, Classic Edition, James 1:2–3 teaches us to be joyful in all kinds of trials because they "bring out endurance and steadfastness and patience." Note that this says trials "bring out" patience, but in my life, they brought a lot of other qualities out of me long before they brought patience. They brought out self-pity, discouragement, anger, reasoning, a loss of peace, and other ungodly traits. I see now that this was good for me because the trials forced me to get to know myself as I really was, not just as I *thought* I was. I thought I was a woman of faith, and I viewed myself as much stronger than I proved to be when tested. God helped me to deal with each of my unpleasant attitudes and eventually to overcome them. And finally, we did get to patience.

To be patient means to be long spirited, and patience means long-suffering with mildness, gentleness, moderation, and constancy. These definitions make sense in light of everything else I have learned about patience. God wants us to be constant, meaning to be the same in difficult times as we are in good times, even if we are going through suffering.

> God wants you to be constant, even if you are suffering.

The word *long-suffering* is a synonym for *patience*, and as you can probably see, it means to be willing to suffer a long time. Therefore, patience is not a pleasant feeling. Patience is a decision to remain calm and pleasant during adversity. In the past two hours, as I have been trying to write about patience, I have received many phone calls that required action on my part. My daughter happened to be in the house when the last call came in, and I said to her, "If my phone rings one more time, I'm going to throw it through the window!" I admit that this didn't sound very patient. I did have the option of simply not answering the phone. I could have returned the calls later when I wasn't writing, but for some reason, many people, including me, cannot seem to let a call go without finding out what the other person wants. The caller doesn't know they are interrupting us, so actually we are the ones who cause the problem.

Sometimes the devil keeps pushing and pushing us until he finally nudges us over the edge. Each time he does, hopefully we learn something from the experience, and I believe God gives us the capacity to handle more the next time. I am determined to have a positive attitude toward everything that happens to me and, with God's help, to continue growing in patience. I have not arrived, but I will not give up.

What Happens When We Are Not Patient?

Luke 21:19 says, "By your patience possess your souls" (NKJV). If you don't possess your soul (mind, will, and emotions), it will possess you. Your mind will rule you, your emotions will rule you, and your own will (power to choose) will end up controlling you instead of your using it to control yourself. We are to be spiritual and to let the Holy Spirit lead us, not allowing our mind, will, and emotions to dictate our lives.

When we are not patient, we are frustrated most of the time. *To frustrate* means "to prevent (a plan or attempted action) from progressing, succeeding, or being fulfilled."[19] Frustration occurs when we try to do something about a situation we can't do anything about, when we try to make something happen that only God can make happen, when we don't have the ability to get something we don't have, or when we try to get rid of something we do have and no matter what we do, it doesn't go away.

> Frustration occurs when you try to make something happen that only God can make happen.

When we are not patient, we often get into works of the flesh, which are our bright ideas and plans for getting what we want through our human effort—and getting it *now*—without waiting on God to come through for us. I call these works of the flesh "works that don't work" because God is not in them. They actually interrupt and delay God's process. When we get involved in them, I've learned that He tends to postpone what He had planned and waits for us to realize that our plans won't succeed without His blessing. Faith is "the leaning of your entire human personality" on God "in absolute trust and confidence in His power, wisdom, and goodness" (Colossians 1:4 AMPC). God waits for us to lean entirely on Him. We are not to be passive as we go through life; we should only take action as God leads us, not just when we feel like it.

> God waits for you to lean entirely on Him.

For example, let's imagine that I want my husband to do something I haven't been able to get him to do, so I've been praying that God will help him see things my way. (This is probably not a good way to pray.) Nothing seems to be happening, so I decide to try to convince Dave one more time, which ends up making him more resistant than he already was. Now I have to wait even longer for God to move on my behalf.

Ecclesiastes 7:8 says: "Better is the end of a thing than the beginning of it, and the patient in spirit is better than the proud in spirit" (AMPC). People who are proud take matters into their own hands and do their own thing, but God is pleased when we obey His commands—not when we do our own thing and expect Him to make it work for us. We should pray, get God's guidance, and *then* plan, instead of making our own plan and then praying it works.

> *When you are impatient, you forfeit peace and joy.*

When we are impatient, we forfeit our peace and joy. Impatience causes us to feel upset and that is not God's will for us. The kingdom of God is "righteousness and peace and joy in the Holy Spirit" (Romans 14:17 AMP).

I've been saying that we can be blessed in the messes of our lives if we do things God's way, and patience is God's way. Impatience causes stress, and stress causes sickness. A person who does not wait well will eventually see the results in their physical body. According to the Cleveland Clinic,[20] stress can affect us physically in the following ways:

> *Impatience causes stress, and stress causes sickness.*

- Aches and pains
- Chest pain or a feeling like your heart is racing
- Exhaustion or trouble sleeping
- Headaches, dizziness, or shaking
- High blood pressure
- Muscle tension or jaw clenching

- Stomach or digestive problems
- Sexual problems
- Weak immune system

According to the Mayo Clinic,[21] stress can also affect us mentally and emotionally in the following ways:

- Anxiety
- Restlessness
- Lack of motivation or focus
- Feeling overwhelmed
- Irritability or anger
- Sadness or depression

Consider these questions about how you handle stress:

- How do you act while waiting in a line that is moving *very* slowly?
- How do you behave when another driver does something you think is stupid?
- How do you act when you're in a hurry to meet a deadline and you have computer problems?
- How do you act in a huge traffic jam due to an accident?
- How do you respond when circumstances don't go your way?

I want to share a few situations that cause stress in my life and ask you to think about how you feel when you encounter circumstances like them:

- How do you act when someone doesn't understand your instructions the first time you give them, and you have to tell that person again and again? This one is a weakness for me.

- How do you act when you ask someone for something, and they give you something totally different? Dave and I often order food to go and take it home to eat. I can definitely say that at least half of the time, something is wrong with the order. The meal wasn't what we ordered, something was forgotten, or it was packaged poorly and ended up in the bottom of the bag. We once ordered a double cheeseburger for Dave, and when we got home, we discovered it had no cheese. I thought that was bad until a friend told me he ordered a cheeseburger from the same restaurant, and when he started to eat it, he found it had no burger or cheese—just bread, pickles and condiments. We have now reached the point where, when we order takeout, we actually unpack the meal before we leave the restaurant to make sure it is correct. When it isn't, we have to wait some more while they make it right. We've even had to send food back two or three times. I'm feeling impatient just telling you about what we sometimes go through to get the meals we've ordered.
- What do you do when you want to buy something but know you should wait and save the money for it instead of charging it to a credit card that's nearly maxed out? Does impatience cause you to go deeper into debt and go against your conscience?

I only ask these questions to get you to think. I have had to deal with every one of these situations and still do on occasion. If you deal with them also, believe me when I say that I understand.

I have learned to choose not to let every inconvenience stress me out. If we allow ourselves to get worked up over everything we don't like, the stress will become too much and eventually harm our health. I hope you'll make the decision to grow in patience when you're tempted to feel stressed. It will help you stay at peace, and it will be good for your health.

Enjoy the Moment

God wants us to enjoy the time He gives us, and every moment we waste is one we will never get back. Patience allows us to enjoy the present, but impatient people don't enjoy it because they want to get past the current moment and into the next one. Impatient people are never happy with *right now*; they are always going to be happy when something happens that they have been looking forward to. I believe one of life's greatest tragedies is being upset about what we don't have while not enjoying what we do have.

> *Being upset about what you don't have while not enjoying what you do have is one of life's great tragedies.*

Impatient people rush and hurry all the time, even when they aren't going anywhere specific. A patient person is a powerful person. The Bible says that it's better to be a patient person with self-control than a warrior who can take an entire city in battle (Proverbs 16:32).

Each moment we have is truly a gift from God, and not to enjoy it is tragic. The moments we miss often hold miracles we miss— perhaps the miracle of a flower in full bloom, or the miracle of hearing what God is trying to say to us, or the miracle of changing a life through showing kindness. We miss moments like these because we are in too much of a hurry to even notice them.

I've heard that the greatest present we can ever have is the present. It is the moment we have, never knowing if it will be our last. I desperately need this chapter I am writing, so if you don't, then I am happy to write it just for myself. I need to be reminded of these things in order to stay on the right path. Patience has to be practiced and practiced and practiced. Some people are more patient than others due to their temperament. Dave is one of those people, and I am not, so I have to try a little—well, let's be honest—I have to try *a lot* more than he does.

Much of life is ordinary. In fact, most of life is ordinary. And during our ordinary days, messy things happen sometimes. When they do, we can exercise patience in the messes by letting the world do whatever it will while we remain stable and happy. Patient people are thankful for the good things in their life, and they trust God to work out everything else for their good.

People who are patient enjoy everything they do, even tasks that would not ordinarily be enjoyable. It is their attitude that allows them to enjoy these things. Their tasks may not be fun, but when people are patient, they can have joy while doing them because they have made a decision to do so.

Never Give Up

People who have developed patience refuse to give up, no matter how many times they have to try something before they finally succeed. They don't give up on people who need to change either. They keep praying and believing that God is working and that they will eventually see change.

The world is full of successful people who failed many times before they succeeded. Why? Because they never gave up. Many of them had no special talent; they were simply determined.

Enjoy reading this story about the spider and the king.

The Spider and the King

Hundreds of years ago, things were not going well for Robert the Bruce, King of Scotland. His country was losing a war with England, and many of his soldiers had been captured. Eventually, the king was forced to hide in a cave, trying to escape the English army. When he received word that his wife and daughter had been taken prisoner and his brothers had been killed, he decided to give up and die in the cave.

He soon noticed a spider spinning its web across the roof of the cave. He watched the spider hang a bridge line on which to secure its web, then swing back and forth across the roof to attach each strand of the web to a portion of the cave roof and walls. Many times, the spider tried to swing to the other side and missed. He began to count and realized the spider had swung six times trying to attach one thread. And six times, it had failed.

The king spoke to the spider, saying, "Little spider, you may as well give up, like me." But the spider kept trying. It worked harder and harder until finally, it landed where it wanted to be.

When the king realized that the spider failed six times, but succeeded on its seventh try, he stood and declared, "And for Scotland, I will win, too!" He left the cave, began to gather and inspire soldiers to fight with him, and after a gallant battle, eventually drove the English out of Scotland.

The king then made a treaty with England and released the English soldiers he had captured. The English let the king's wife and daughter go, and they returned to their home in Scotland, with the king. Later, King Robert's son married the daughter of the king of England, and the two countries lived in peace. King Robert never forgot the lesson of perseverance he learned from the little spider in the cave.[22]

Why should a spider have more patience than you and I do? The king was depressed after being defeated, but after witnessing the spider's determination, he decided to keep trying until he succeeded. For the remainder of the story, nothing else is mentioned about his being depressed. We feel depressed when we give up, but activity and hope fill us with happiness.

We need to refuse to be trapped in our past or present problems. We usually need to get a new attitude before we see our circumstances change. The Bible says that new wine cannot be poured into old wineskins (Mark 2:22). One way to look at this scripture is to say that a

> *Refuse to be trapped in your past or present problems.*

new life won't fit into old thinking. Change your mind and change your attitude—and a changed life will follow.

Giving up is easy. Anyone can give up, but it takes strength and determination to keep going when the journey is long and hard. Trust that the way God leads you, whatever way it may be, is the best way. And trust that His timing in your life is perfect.

We all have plans and ideas about the way we think things should work out in our lives. But if what we planned doesn't work out, or even if what God had originally planned doesn't work out due to human error, He always has a new and better plan. God doesn't give up, so why should we? God is extraordinarily patient.

God had a plan for Saul to be king of Israel, and he was king for a period of time. But Saul was rebellious and wouldn't wait on God. At one point, the prophet Samuel told him not to offer a sacrifice before going to war until he, Samuel, arrived. He also told him he would have to wait for him for seven days at a place called Gilgal (1 Samuel 10:8). Before the end of the seventh day, Saul's soldiers began to leave, so Saul offered the sacrifice anyway (1 Samuel 13:8–9). His impatience caused him to lose the kingdom.

As Samuel mourned the loss of Saul, God asked him how long he was going to mourn after He had rejected Saul as king. He said,

"Fill your horn with oil and be on your way; I am sending you
to Jesse of Bethlehem. I have chosen one of his sons to be king"
(1 Samuel 16:1). Saul failed, but God had a new and better plan,
which was for David to be anointed king.

When we fail, if we continue trusting God, He will always have
a new plan. Stop looking at your past and start looking at your
future. Never give up until you are enjoying the life that Jesus
died to give you.

Help in Building Patience

Meditating on Scripture helps us do what God wants us to do,
and He does want us to grow in patience. Here are five scriptures related to patience for you to read, think about, and meditate on.

> Be joyful in hope, patient in affliction, faithful in prayer.
>
> Romans 12:12

> Let us not become weary in doing good, for at the proper
> time we will reap a harvest if we do not give up.
>
> Galatians 6:9

> Be completely humble and gentle; be patient, bearing with
> one another in love.
>
> Ephesians 4:2

> Be still before the Lord and wait patiently for him; do not
> fret when people succeed in their ways, when they carry
> out their wicked schemes. Refrain from anger and turn
> from wrath; do not fret—it leads only to evil. For those

who are evil will be destroyed, but those who hope in the Lord will inherit the land.

Psalm 37:7–9

Therefore, as God's chosen people, holy and dearly loved, clothe yourselves with compassion, kindness, humility, gentleness and patience.

Colossians 3:12

CHAPTER 11

Be Thankful

If the only prayer you ever say in your entire life is thank you, it will be enough.

Meister Eckhart[23]

I have mentioned that God will bless us in our mess if we do things His way, and if we want to succeed and be blessed in life, we cannot ignore the importance of a thankful attitude. Our lives need to be filled with thanksgiving. The more grateful we are, the more powerful our prayers are and the less access our spiritual enemy, Satan, has to our lives.

> *Your life needs to be filled with thanksgiving.*

I have often said that I think walking in love is a form of spiritual warfare, and I also believe that being thankful is a way to wage war against the enemy. I am fond of this phrase from Psalm 100:4: "Be thankful and say so to Him" (AMPC). We may consider ourselves to be thankful, but do we say so? If not, we need to tell both God and people that we are thankful for them and for what they do for us.

I believe that one positive way trials and trouble affect us is to make us thankful for the good things in our lives. If everything in our life is good all the time, we begin to take it for granted and lose our appreciation for it.

> *If everything in life were good all the time, you might take it for granted.*

Even in the midst of our worst problems, all of us can find things to be thankful for. You may not like your job or some of the people you work with, but you can still be thankful you have a job and remember that there are many unemployed people who would love to have the work you may complain about. You might not like some of the things your employer does, but the situation could be worse. At this moment, you may be frustrated with your spouse, but there are probably lonely people everywhere who would gladly trade the inherent challenges of close relationships for the loneliness of solitude.

Be Thankful on Purpose

Complaining happens automatically if we don't commit ourselves to intentional thankfulness. Our flesh is always ready to complain about something, but this does not lead to blessing. There are hundreds of scriptures in the Bible about thanksgiving and being thankful. One of my favorite ones is this:

> Do not fret or have any anxiety about anything, but in every circumstance and in everything, by prayer and petition (definite requests), with thanksgiving, continue to make your wants known to God.
>
> Philippians 4:6 AMPC

When we are worried, God gives us the privilege of praying in every circumstance and making our wants known to Him. But He tells us to do so *with thanksgiving*. If we are not thankful for what we already have, we are not ready for anything else. Thankful people are humble people who don't have an attitude of entitlement, but one of gratitude.

There are literally thousands of things all around us for which we can be thankful if we will simply look for them. What about air to breathe? We may have never thanked God for it, but people with lung problems are grateful for every breath they can take. How about color? Just imagine how boring life would look if everything were black, white, and gray. Did you drive in traffic today and make it to your destination safely? If so, this is a reason to be thankful.

In the United States, most people have clean, hot and cold running water in their homes, yet in many parts of the world, people walk miles each day just to take home dirty, disease-ridden water because that is all they have.

You may be stuck in traffic at times, but your heat or air-conditioning is probably on, depending on the weather outside. You can be thankful you are in a car instead of waiting at a bus stop in bad weather. Have you eaten today? Many people in the world have not.

The list of reasons to be thankful can go on and on. But when inconvenience comes our way, our first impulse is to complain unless we determine to be thankful on purpose.

My family and I were recently on our way to the airport when we found out our flight was delayed for five hours. I admit that my first impulse was to murmur, but my daughter, sitting next to me in the car, quickly said, "All things work together for good. God may be saving us from a bad accident." I calmed down immediately, and we made plans to spend the time waiting for our flight doing some things that turned out to be enjoyable. You see, if we keep a good, thankful attitude, it opens the door for God to turn a problem into a blessing. But if we complain, it opens a door for the devil to make the problem worse than it already is.

I know someone who has terminal cancer, and she has a better attitude than many perfectly healthy people I know. She has decided that she is not going to spend her last few months on earth complaining, and I really admire her for this.

I have made the decision to be thankful, but I have to keep making it each day. I do well with thanksgiving for a while, then something happens that I don't like, and I complain, have to repent, and then recommit myself to being thankful. But I know if I keep at it and don't give up, I will reach my goal of living a thankful life, because I see progress on a regular basis.

When you want to form a new habit in your life, don't be discouraged about how far you have to go. Be encouraged about how far you have come as you're making progress, little by little.

What Is God's Will for My Life?

One of the questions people frequently ask me is "What is God's will for my life?" I realize they are often asking what specifically God wants them to do as a career or in a certain situation, but let's think about God's will in a different way. The apostle Paul writes:

> Thank [God] in everything [no matter what the circumstances may be, be thankful and give thanks], for this is the will of God for you [who are] in Christ Jesus [the Revealer and Mediator of that will]. Do not quench (suppress or subdue) the [Holy] Spirit.
>
> 1 Thessalonians 5:18–19 AMPC

These verses tell us that God's will is for us to be thankful in everything, no matter what our circumstance may be. If we are not being thankful in every situation, how can we expect the Holy Spirit to guide us into God's specific will for our lives? If we are not thankful, we quench or suppress the Holy Spirit. If you have questions about God's will for your life and don't seem to be getting any answers, ask yourself how thankful you are. If you are lacking in this area, sincerely increase your gratitude, and you will probably sense the Holy Spirit's guidance more clearly.

Increase your gratitude, and you will sense the Holy Spirit's guidance more clearly.

I think being grateful in all circumstances is quite challenging. We may have to keep working at it with God's help for the rest of our lives. How can we thank God for everything no matter what the circumstance may be? What if the circumstance is extremely difficult—such as the death of a loved one, the loss of a job, or an accident that leaves you impaired for life? The only way I believe we can remain thankful through such situations is to believe Romans 8:28, which teaches us that God will work all things for our good if we continue to love Him and want His will. Circumstances don't have to be positive in order for God to make something good out of them. If we absolutely cannot find a way to thank God *for* the situation we are in, then in the midst of it we can at least thank Him for other good things He is doing and tell Him that we trust Him to work out the current circumstance in a positive way.

The psalmist David writes, "I will extol the Lord *at all times*; his praise will always be on my lips" (Psalm 34:1, emphasis mine). When he says, "I will," he is using strong words. They refer to making a decision and a commitment. This verse comes across as though David is determined not to talk about his feelings, but to extol or praise God, and we would be wise to follow his example.

Thank God Repeatedly for the Same Things

Don't get tired of thanking God for the same things over and over again. We thank God for our food at every meal, so why not do the same with other blessings He gives us? Paul writes to the believers in the church at Philippi: "I thank my God every time I remember you. In all my prayers for all of you, I always pray with joy because of your partnership in the gospel from the first day until now" (Philippians 1:3–5). He didn't just thank God for them once or twice; he prayed for them every time they came to mind.

You and I can pray the same prayers repeatedly too. Don't ever stop thanking God for giving Jesus to pay for your sins. Don't ever stop thanking Him for sending the Holy Spirit to live in you. If you are healthy, thank Him daily for your good health and strength, because it is miserable to be sick all the time. I've had periods of time when I've been sick, and I can tell you that feeling well is much, much better. If you have family and friends who love you, it's a reason to be thankful, because the world is full of lonely people. Believe me when I say that you will not run out of things to be thankful for if you look for them.

I don't think we should ever take our petitions (requests) to God without first thanking Him for what He has already done for us. The Bible says we enter His gates with thanksgiving (Psalm 100:4). If we take this literally, it means we cannot even come into God's presence without thanksgiving.

Anytime you start to feel depressed or discouraged, start thanking God for the blessings in your life. You can stop the attacks of the enemy with gratitude. According to Psalm 106:14, the Israelites lusted after many things while they were in the wilderness. Psalm 106:16 also says they were envious of Moses and Aaron. If they were greedy and jealous, they couldn't have been thankful. We should not covet and be envious of other people. God has an individual plan for each of us, and we need to trust that His plan for us is perfect. If we are not getting what we want right now, He has a reason for not releasing it yet.

One of the worst things that can happen to a person is to get something that is not part of God's will for them or that comes outside of His perfect timing. The Israelites were tired of the manna God gave them daily, and they lusted for meat. When God gave it to them, they ate so much that they got sick (Numbers 11:4–6, 31–34). Sometimes we think we know what we want, and God has to give it to us in order for us to realize that it isn't what we want after all.

Thankful People Are Happy People

A person who is thankful is well liked. On the other hand, no matter how much someone likes you, they will get tired of being around you if you complain all the time. In addition to being thankful to God, we should thank the people who do things for us. Saying thank you takes only a few seconds, but it goes a long way in keeping relationships strong. Everyone wants to feel appreciated. It keeps people encouraged. When people feel appreciated, they want to do even more for you than they are already doing.

If I am good to someone or do a lot for them and never hear them say thank you, it tells me a lot about their character and lets me know that they are spiritually immature. Form a habit of thanking people for even the most minor favor or blessing. The more thankful you are, the happier you will be.

A thankful person also focuses on the positive aspects of life— not the negative ones. And being positive always opens the door for joy. We all want to be happy, and we often make the mistake of thinking we will be happy if we can just get everything we want. But this is not true. The truth is that we will be happy when we become thankful for what we do have. Things or possessions are nice to have, but they have no lasting ability to keep us happy. Things lose their luster quickly, and then we want a new thing, hoping that one will make us happy. Until we learn to enjoy things but not depend on them for our happiness, we will always be chasing another new thing.

I remember being in a jewelry store one time and seeing some jewelry that was absolutely beautiful. I bought a couple of pieces, and when I got them home, they didn't look nearly as nice as they did in the store. Then I realized that the lights shining on them in the jewelry case at the store had made them look so irresistible. I took them back and got a refund, but I also learned a lesson to not buy things based on emotion, because no matter how good they looked when I got them, they didn't stay that way.

I like nice things, and there is nothing wrong with having them as long as you can afford them and are not being excessive.

I also know without a doubt that my joy doesn't come from things outside of me; it comes from having Jesus in my life and being thankful.

Symptoms of a Lack of Gratitude

When people are sneezing, coughing, and blowing their nose, they have symptoms of allergies or a cold. If they are complaining, murmuring, and finding fault with their life, they have symptoms of an attitude of ingratitude. It is easy to spot an ungrateful person. Just watch for the symptoms, which include:

- negativity
- complaining
- selfishness
- an attitude of entitlement
- comparison
- jealousy
- pride
- self-pity

It is good to watch for the symptoms of ingratitude in ourselves. We can think, *I am grateful*, yet in reality, we are not grateful at all. We can easily deceive ourselves. Jeremiah 17:9 says: "The heart is deceitful above all things, and desperately wicked; who can know it?" (NKJV). If I say I am thankful but complain frequently or am jealous of what other people have that I don't, then in reality, I am not truly thankful.

We all want to think we are good people and that we do all the right things, but the proof is in the pudding, so to speak. We see more about ourselves through what we do than through the way we think about ourselves. It is a little scary to realize how easily we can deceive ourselves into thinking we are better than

we are. This is why asking God to

> *It is easy to deceive yourself*
> *into thinking you are better*
> *than you are.*

reveal truth to us on a regular basis is good.

It is also good to watch for situations that let us know if we really are who we think we are. For example, I think I am an extremely thankful person, but then I hear myself complaining about something and know I still need to increase in gratitude. We should be thankful when God shows us any area of our life that isn't what it should be, because we cannot fix something if we don't know it is broken.

I admit that I sometimes hear myself complaining and then repent and realize I still have lots of room to grow in this all-important area of gratitude. I did a lot of complaining last week while trying to deal with our insurance company about a prescription they didn't want to cover for me, even though my doctor had ordered it. This was very confusing to me. They finally sent the medicine but charged me $1,500 for it when it should have been only an $8 copayment. So, it took several more calls and sitting on the phone waiting for someone to talk to me before I convinced them they owed me a refund.

I also complain about taxes. It seems almost everything has a tax added to it. About the only thing I can think of that you don't have to pay tax on is being born, but if someone thinks of it, even that could become a reality. What we have left when we die is taxed (called the death tax), and there is sales tax, federal and state income tax, city tax, real estate tax, gasoline tax, hotel tax, personal property tax, social security tax, gift tax, capital gains tax, excise tax, value added tax, and probably more.

I guess I am having a confession session right now, but having one occasionally is probably good for all of us. At least I am growing in my awareness of my tendency to complain about these areas of my life. I suppose I could thank God I have something to pay taxes on.

Let's celebrate God's goodness and ask Him to forgive us for all the times we fail to see and be thankful for all He does for us.

CHAPTER 12

Believe That God Is Bigger Than Your Problems

If you give it to God, He transforms your test into a testimony, your mess into a message, and your misery into a ministry.

Rick Warren[24]

W hat comes into our minds when we think about God is the most important thing about us," wrote A. W. Tozer in his 1961 book, *The Knowledge of the Holy*.[25] The way we think and what we believe can help us or defeat us. Do you believe God is greater than your problems? Do you believe all things are possible with Him?

God is greater than any problem or enemy we have. When the Bible speaks of enemies, it often refers to literal enemies, because throughout Scripture we read of people and groups who were set against God's people and out to harm them. Sometimes, though, our enemies are the troubles or difficulties we face.

I have seen God defeat my enemies when they threatened to defeat me many times. I've also observed this in the lives of other people. As I read Scripture, I also see God showing Himself to be greater than the problems of many people we read about in the Bible.

God was greater than David's sin with Bathsheba and the murder of her husband, because He forgave and restored them (2 Samuel chapters 11 and 12). He was greater than Peter's denial of His Son, Jesus Christ (Luke 22:54–62). He was greater than Paul's imprisonment (Acts 16:16–40), and greater than the sins of Rahab the prostitute (Joshua 2; 6:17–25; Hebrews 11:31; James 2:25).

In each of these cases, the people who sinned repented of their sin, and God forgave their sin and brought restoration into their lives. He did not discard them but continued to use them for His glory. Romans 5:20 says, "Where sin increased, grace abounded all the more" (ESV). God's goodness is greater than anything wrong that we can do.

The reason I am so convinced that God is greater than anything we may face is that 1 John 4:4 says, "He who is in you is greater than he who is in the world" (NKJV). As believers, Jesus lives in us. The devil is in the world, and he does have power, but he doesn't have more power than God, who lives in us by His Spirit.

Over more than forty-five years of serving God, I have dealt with many problems—big ones as well as smaller ones. I can say with assurance that God has shown Himself greater than all of them. He didn't always act when I would have liked for Him to or the way I thought He would, but He has always been faithful.

Here are a few scriptures about the power and greatness of God:

> He heals the brokenhearted and binds up their wounds. He determines the number of the stars; he gives to all of them their names. Great is our Lord, and abundant in power; his understanding is beyond measure.
>
> Psalm 147:3–5 (ESV)

> He who is the blessed and only Sovereign, the King of kings and Lord of lords, who alone has immortality, who dwells in unapproachable light, whom no one has ever seen or can see. To him be honor and eternal dominion. Amen.
>
> 1 Timothy 6:15–16 (ESV)

> But Jesus looked at them and said, "With man this is impossible, but with God all things are possible."
>
> Matthew 19:26 (ESV)

> Behold, I am the Lord, the God of all flesh. Is anything too hard for me?
>
> Jeremiah 32:27 (ESV)

God Loves Us and He Is Good

I think that before we can trust God to take care of all of our problems and depend on Him to deliver us, we must believe that He loves us and that He is always good. As far as I am concerned, these are foundational truths that cement our relationship with God. Consider these scriptures:

> For God so loved the world that he gave his one and only Son, that whoever believes in him shall not perish but have eternal life.
>
> John 3:16

> But God demonstrates his own love for us in this: While we were still sinners, Christ died for us.
>
> Romans 5:8

> No, in all these things we are more than conquerors through him who loved us. For I am convinced that neither death nor life, neither angels nor demons, neither the present nor the future, nor any powers, neither height nor depth, nor anything else in all creation, will be able to separate us from the love of God that is in Christ Jesus our Lord.
>
> Romans 8:37–39

No problem is big enough to separate you from God's love.

No problem is big enough to separate us from God's love. It keeps us strong and full of hope and faith in the worst of circumstances. When we are totally confident of God's love, no problem can keep us from it.

God's Love Defeats Your Enemies

If we truly believe God loves us, we can also truly believe He will keep us safe and help us in every situation. When I experience disturbing problems, one thing I do while I am waiting for God to deliver me is to say often, "I know You love me, Lord." This reminds me of His love, and it is also a decla-

> *Declaring the Word of God does damage to Satan's plan of destruction.*

ration of my faith. Each time we declare the Word of God, it does damage to Satan's plan of destruction.

We face many different kinds of problems. In saying that God is greater than our problems, we should consider the problems that attack our soul in addition to those that affect our physical body or our circumstances. For example, lack of finances is a problem, but so is fear. Being physically sick is a problem, but so is being insecure.

God's love is the answer to fear, insecurity, and many other problems of the heart and soul. "Perfect love casts out fear" (1 John 4:18 NKJV). Only God can love us perfectly and unconditionally. It is His love that heals our brokenness. Because my father abused me and my mother abandoned me to his abuse, I never experienced real love until I learned how to receive God's love. Dave loved me, but I didn't believe I was loveable for a long time, so I did not receive his love. Until we allow the love of God to heal our souls, we can't receive love from anyone else, because we don't believe we are loveable.

God has proven to me that He is greater than everything that has come against me. No matter what people do to you or life does to you, God is greater. He is also great enough to work out for your good everything that happens to you (Romans 8:28).

God Is Good at All Times

I believe beyond any doubt or question that God is good, so even in the midst of painful situations, I have confidence that His goodness will bring healing to my life.

We can only see God's goodness because of the things in life that are not good. I love this statement by Jonathan Edwards: "There would be no manifestation of God's grace or true goodness, if there was no sin to be pardoned, no misery to be saved from."[26]

When I sin and God completely forgives me and even forgets my sin (Hebrews 10:17), I see His goodness. If I am sick and He heals me, I see His goodness. Yesterday for some reason I felt bad all day. This morning when I woke up, I felt all better and I kept thanking God over and over. My heart was full of thanksgiving for His love and goodness because I was experiencing it in my life.

God is good all the time, but we often become so accustomed to His goodness that we fail to notice it. This is one reason a little trouble can be beneficial to us. It lets us see how life would be without the goodness of God.

Pray to see God's goodness in your life. And remember Matthew 7:11: "If you then, being evil, know how to give good gifts to your children, how much more will your Father who is in heaven give good things to those who ask Him!" (NKJV).

Watch Your Enemies Flee

Instead of running from our enemies (again, meaning the troubles we face), we can watch them run from us. Deuteronomy 28:7 says, "The Lord will cause your enemies who rise against you to be defeated before your face; they shall come out against you one way and flee before you seven ways" (NKJV). And in Exodus 23:22

God promises to be an enemy to our enemies and an adversary to our adversaries if we obey Him.

Not only is God greater than your enemies, but *you* are greater than they are. His Word says, "Behold, I give you the authority to trample on serpents and scorpions, and over all the power of the enemy, and nothing shall by any means hurt you" (Luke 10:19 NKJV).

Because God lives in you, there is no problem you cannot conquer if you are walking in obedience to Him. Submit yourself to God, as James 4:7 teaches, "resist the devil, and he will flee from you."

God Turns Messes into Miracles

I believe the greatest miracle we can witness is watching God change a human being. As I mentioned earlier, at one time in my life, I was a total mess. What God has done in me is a miracle as far as I am concerned. No amount of willpower or human strength could have changed me the way God has changed me. I have witnessed the same amazing changes in countless other people.

> The greatest miracle you can witness is to watch God change a human being.

When we are born again, we become new creatures. The old passes away and all things become brand-new (2 Corinthians 5:17). I like to say that we become new spiritual "clay" for God to work with. Our heart changes immediately, but our behavior doesn't. It goes through a process of transformation. Transformation takes place as our mind is renewed by God's Word. We learn to think like God thinks, and then we can be who He wants us to be. Romans 12:2 says, "Do not conform to the pattern of this world, but be *transformed* by the renewing of your mind. Then you will be able to test and approve what God's will is—his good, pleasing and perfect will" (emphasis mine).

What we believe has a tremendous impact on the way we behave. As we learn to believe God's Word, we are changed into His image, and our behavior reflects these positive changes. According to 2 Corinthians 3:18, "All of us, as with unveiled face, [because we] continued to behold [in the Word of God] as in a mirror the glory of the Lord, *are constantly being transfigured into His very own image* in ever increasing splendor and from one degree of glory to another; [for this comes] from the Lord [Who is] the Spirit" (AMPC, emphasis mine).

I have said repeatedly in this book that God will bless us in the midst of our messes if we do things His way, and I firmly believe it. Studying, learning, and believing His Word is something we need to do to see our messes transformed into miracles.

Many people think they cannot understand God's Word. If this is the case for you, then I recommend you begin by listening to and reading books written by people who have studied it and do understand it. Make sure you learn from a reputable person, because not everyone speaks truth. You can read books about the Bible, and there are countless study books on each book of the Bible that will help you understand what each one teaches and how to apply it to your life. I believe that if you are determined to learn, the Holy Spirit will show you the best pathway to do so, so don't give up.

From a Mess to a Miracle

The transformation of the apostle Paul (formerly Saul) is a good example of a mess that was turned into a miracle. Saul was a very religious man, an expert in the Jewish law, which was written before Christ was born. Saul thought he was doing God's will by persecuting Christians. He thought, as many others did, that Christians were causing trouble and that Jesus was being sacrilegious by referring to Himself as God. He feared that if Christians were allowed to spread their message, many Jews would be deceived. He thought persecuting the Christians would please God, because he had not yet encountered Jesus. Paul was sincere, but he was sincerely wrong.

One day, Jesus appeared to Saul in a dramatic way as he traveled from Jerusalem to Damascus. You can read this story, along with some of what happened after Saul's conversion in Acts 9:1–31. But for now, let me simply say that as a result of his encounter with Jesus, in which his name was changed from Saul to Paul, he was transformed into a great apostle of Christ who wrote approximately two-thirds of the New Testament and took the gospel message to the Gentiles, whom he formerly despised.

No matter how bad a person is, one encounter with the living Christ can transform them into a totally different person, as happened with Saul. My father was one of the meanest men I ever met, and after he surrendered his life to Christ at the age of eighty-three, I saw a true transformation in him. He became sweet, and although he had always used offensive and filthy language, I never heard him do it again.

You can have hope for yourself if you need to be changed, and you can have hope for any of your friends or loved ones who need to change. You can't change people, but you can pray for them, and God can change them.

To begin this chapter, I quoted Rick Warren: "If you give it to God, He transforms your test into a testimony, your mess into a message, and your misery into a ministry." How could we ever have a testimony that encourages others if we never have a test? I often say that many people, after having a test, don't have a testimony; they only have the "*moanies*." They moan, murmur, and complain about the discomfort so much that they never give God an opportunity to show Himself strong in their life.

If you have big messes (troubles, trials, tribulations) in your life, make this the moment that you ask God to take them and turn them into blessings. He not only *can* do it; He *wants* to do it. He will show you what you need to do, if anything. As you are obedient to Him and do what you can do, He will do what you cannot do.

Take the time to slowly digest this Scripture passage and remember that it is one of God's promises to you:

> So do not fear, for I am with you; do not be dismayed, for I am your God. I will strengthen you and help you; I will uphold you with my righteous right hand. All who rage against you will surely be ashamed and disgraced; those who oppose you will be as nothing and perish. Though you search for your enemies, you will not find them. Those who wage war against you will be as nothing at all. For I am the Lord your God who takes hold of your right hand and says to you, Do not fear; I will help you.
>
> Isaiah 41:10–13

| *Your problem can make you stronger.* |

Wow! If you believe these words, you can start rejoicing right now. God will take what Satan meant for harm and turn it into something good (Genesis 50:20). Your problem can make you stronger.

No Weapon Formed against Me Shall Succeed

God says in Isaiah 54:17, "No weapon forged against you will prevail, and you will refute every tongue that accuses you. This is the heritage of the servants of the Lord, and this is their vindication from me."

This verse reminds us again that our enemies are not greater than God. Even when people come against us unjustly, they will be shown to be in the wrong. God will vindicate us (Psalm 54:1). Our part is to forgive them and pray for them and then to sit back and watch God work (Matthew 5:44). It may take time, perhaps even years, but it will happen if we continue to trust God and obey His Word.

One of the most devastating and painful things that has happened to me during my ministry was caused by people I truly thought were my best friends. They turned against me and accused me of things I did not do. They deserted me at a crucial time in my life. It took me about three years to get over the shock and devastation of this situation. Many years passed before I heard an apology, but eventually one did come.

It hurts when people you trust and love betray you. This happened to Jesus with Judas (Matthew 26:14–16), and it happened to Paul at his first trial. He wrote in 2 Timothy 4:16: "At my first defense, no one came to my support, but everyone deserted me. May it not be held against them."

This verse indicates that Paul continued walking in love with those who deserted him and even asked God not to hold it against them. When Jesus was on the cross, suffering agony we cannot even imagine, He asked God to forgive those who crucified Him, saying that they didn't know what they were doing (Luke 23:34). And when Stephen, a martyr in the early church, was being stoned for his faith in God, he asked God to forgive those who were stoning him (Acts 7:59–60). If you have some people in your life that are hard to love, I recommend my book *Loving People Who Are Hard to Love.*

If you and I will pray for the people who hurt us, God will take our pain and turn it into our gain. With God on our side, we always win over our enemies in the end.

CHAPTER 13

Trust God When You Don't Understand

A person who lives in faith must proceed on incomplete evidence, trusting in advance what will only make sense in reverse.

Philip Yancey[27]

A friend and coworker shared this story with me:

I went through a time when I was angry at God. Very angry. And instead of dealing with it, I marinated in it. I sat and stewed in the juices of disappointment and rage.

You see, I had gone through several terrible situations in succession, including an incredibly difficult false accusation that cut me to the core, and the shocking loss of someone I loved dearly to suicide.

My entire life had been built on trusting God, and ironically, a part of my job was to share stories of amazing things God has done. So, I knew that God answered prayer. I had seen it over and over. I knew that He could even do the miraculous. Yet in the circumstances that were casting a shadow over my life, God was silent. He didn't intervene, and the worst happened.

I was devastated. I felt like my life was in shambles while God looked the other way, and I was furious.

At first, being angry felt good. It scratched the itch to somehow make someone pay. I thought I deserved to be angry. But anger is a liar. It is never healing; it is an infection that sets in and makes a wound even worse—festering and spreading to other parts of our life.

I took out my revenge on the only one who could help me and slammed the door on His healing love and blessings. I became more and more angry, distant, and hopeless. I was a mess. Eventually I just couldn't stand it anymore. I remember lying on the floor in my living room and crying inconsolably. I asked God where He had been when these devastating things were happening to me, and after the floodgate of tears subsided, I felt a warmth come over me and had the distinct feeling that He had been there waiting for me all along.

Like a stubborn little girl, I had been pouting in my room instead of running to my Father's arms. Through my anger and disobedience, He was there whenever I was ready.

Through tears, I told Him how sorry I was for thinking I knew better than He did. I was still hurting, and my circumstances hadn't changed, but I couldn't keep up the anger any longer. It was eating me alive. Almost immediately, when I surrendered it all to Him, asked Him to forgive me, and told Him how much I needed His help, I felt a release and a beautiful peace.

I hated the things I was going through, but I was worse off in my hopelessness than in giving it all to God and embracing the hope that only He can offer. That's when the healing began. That's when, even in my brokenness, I saw God slowly but surely bring joy back into my world and set my feet on firmer ground.

Now, years later, I can see how God took terrible things, things that He did not cause to happen but chose to love me through, and He tenderly healed, restored, and taught me.

Today I have such empathy for people who have experienced the devastation of suicide and loss. I'm not so quick to judge or believe every story I hear about people, either.

I know that God can take our questions, doubt, and anger, and gently love us through them. And I am better and more grateful because of it. In spite of the mess, I have been blessed!

When We Don't Understand

We live life forward, but as Philip Yancey observes in the opening quotation for this chapter, often we can only understand it looking back at things we did not understand while they were happening.

After I quit my job to prepare for the ministry I believed God had called me to, Dave and I went through six years that were lean financially. I thought that because I had made a huge sacrifice to quit my job in order to study God's Word, blessings would come pouring in. But we had fewer financial resources than ever. We continued to tithe on our income, but it was a very confusing and difficult time for me. When we do what is right and don't get what we think is a "right" result, we can become extremely frustrated.

> *You may become frustrated if you do what is right and don't get what you think is the "right" result.*

The six financially difficult years for Dave and me were definitely a test. Would I be willing to serve God even if it meant doing without many things I was accustomed to having? Would I trust Him no matter what? Could I be in need and not be jealous of people who lived life abundantly? God confronted me with these questions and many others like them.

God did take care of us, and somehow each month we were able to pay our bills. But I had to use every coupon I could find when I went grocery shopping, and I developed a lot of what I call "garage sale faith." Each week, I went to garage sales looking for things we needed, such as shoes for our children and household items. I trusted God to help me find what I was looking for, and He did. I am not saying it is wrong to look for bargains at garage sales—it can be fun—but I doubt that any of us want to have to depend on garage sales for the rest of our lives.

Eventually, our financial test did come to an end. I started teaching a weekly Bible study for women at our church. It was so successful and well attended that the pastor gave me a salary of

$65 per week. That $65 looked like $6,000 to me. Eventually, I went to work full-time at the church and once again had a regular income.

While I was going through our six lean years, I had no understanding of why they were important. But as I look back on them, I now know I was learning to trust God when I didn't understand, and I realize that the experience helped me learn to trust God for the finances we now need to operate the worldwide ministry we have.

There is no need at all for faith if we always understand what happens in our lives. As long as we are in relationship with God, we will have some unanswered questions. According to 1 Corinthians 13:9, "we know in part." We don't know everything.

God's ways and thoughts are higher than ours (Isaiah 55:8–9). They are not only higher than ours, but they are better than ours. We may not always understand God's ways, but the way He does things is always much, much better than the way we would do them. Occasionally, I try to give God advice about what He could do to help my situation, but it is a good thing He doesn't listen to me.

> *The way God does things is much better than the way you would do them.*

Romans 11:33 says that God's ways are "past finding out" (NKJV). The Bible talks about the mystery of Christ (Ephesians 3:4; Colossians 4:3), the mystery of the kingdom of God (Mark 4:11 NKJV), and wonders in the heavens (Acts 2:19). It also speaks about the mystery of overcoming death and putting on immortality:

> Listen, I tell you a mystery: We will not all sleep, but we will all be changed—in a flash, in the twinkling of an eye, at the last trumpet. For the trumpet will sound, the dead will be raised imperishable, and we will be changed. For

the perishable must clothe itself with the imperishable, and the mortal with immortality. When the perishable has been clothed with the imperishable, and the mortal with immortality, then the saying that is written will come true: "Death has been swallowed up in victory."

1 Corinthians 15:51–54

In addition to the other mysteries I have mentioned, God's Word also speaks of the mystery of God (Colossians 2:2; Revelation 10:7), the mystery of the union of Christ and the church (Ephesians 5:32), and the mystery of the ages "which is Christ in you, the hope of glory" (Colossians 1:27).

It seems clear to me that if we don't like a good mystery, we are not going to enjoy our relationship with God.

Trust Brings Peace

Having too many questions causes confusion, but trusting God brings peace and joy. Mysteries are called mysteries because they are mysterious; we don't understand them. The Bible includes several concepts I wholeheartedly believe but do not make sense to my mind, such as:

- The Trinity (Matthew 3:16–17; 28:19 and others)
- The incarnation of Christ (Philippians 2:6–7 and others)
- The idea that if we want more, we have to give away some of what we have (Luke 6:38)
- The notion that the first will be last, and the last will be first (Matthew 20:16)

Some portions of Scripture, especially in the Old Testament, leave me shaking my head, but they don't confuse me because I have chosen to trust God. You cannot get confused if you refuse to try to figure things out. There is no harm in pondering something to see if you can begin to understand it, but when it starts to confuse you, it is a sign that you need to stop reasoning and merely trust God.

> *You need to stop reasoning and just trust God.*

There are things I enjoy every day but don't understand. For example:

- I don't understand gravity, but I'm enjoying it right now.
- I don't fully understand the mechanics of breathing, but I am enjoying doing it.
- I don't understand how trees, grass, and flowers can look totally dead and be dormant in the wintertime, then come back to life in the spring and be amazingly beautiful, but I enjoy looking at them.
- I don't understand electricity, but I depend on it and appreciate it.
- I don't understand modern technology, but I use and enjoy it every day.

Why do we have such a desire to understand what is going on in our life? Why do we obsess about the future? I think it's because we like to be in control. We want things to turn out a certain way, and we want to know if they will or not. Most of the time, we don't seek to understand the good things that happen to us. We simply receive them joyfully. But when something we consider to be "bad" happens, we want to know why.

I haven't spent much time trying to figure out why God has allowed me to be on television, but if He took me off, I might try really hard to figure that out. I haven't spent time trying to understand why God has blessed me with such a great family, but if I lost one of them, I'm sure I would have questions.

Even Jesus, as He hung on the cross, asked "Why?" He said, "My God, my God, why have you forsaken me?" (Matthew 27:46). There is no record of God answering Him, but He completely trusted His Father because He said, "Father, into your hands I commit my spirit" (Luke 23:46). Those were the last words He spoke on the cross, and after He spoke them, He died.

For years, I was addicted to reasoning. I couldn't settle down and be peaceful until I thought I had figured out what was going on in my life. Even when I thought I had it all figured out, I usually turned out to be wrong. But simply thinking I knew what was going on gave me peace. I am happy to be able to say that because I have grown in my faith through many experiences God has brought me through, now I can have peace even if I don't know the "why" behind everything that happens. Experience with God is one of the most valuable assets we can have, but gaining it takes time. Just remember that each situation you go through, even though it may be hard, if you don't give up, it will give you experience that helps you build your faith and trust in God.

> Experience with God is one of the most valuable assets you can have.

Jesus once told His disciples, "You do not realize now what I am doing, but later you will understand" (John 13:7). He also told them, "I have still many things to say to you, but you are not able…to grasp them now" (John 16:12 AMPC).

If we knew everything about how God intends to use us, we might be filled with pride. And if we knew all God needs to change in us in order to use us, we might get discouraged and give up. Sometimes, the more we know, the more unhappy we are. So be content to know what God reveals and stay at peace. You can be assured that when you need to know something else, He will give you the understanding you need.

Have you ever had one person tell you that another person was gossiping about you? If so, you were probably happier before you found out about it. We should be wise about what we tell other people and be careful not to tell them things that will steal their joy. We should encourage one another, not discourage one another.

Suffering Leaves Many Questions

Suffering is one of the most difficult experiences to understand. Certain types of suffering, such as severe sickness, the loss of a loved one who is young, and many other hardships, are especially confusing. When God put Adam and Eve in the Garden of Eden, He didn't intend for them to suffer, but He did give one command they were not to disobey. They were not to eat of the tree of the knowledge of good and evil (Genesis 2:16–17). He also gave them free will because He wanted them to love Him because they *chose* to, not because they *had* to. They disobeyed God by doing the one thing He told them not to do, and this brought sin into the world (Genesis 3:1–21; Romans 5:12–19). When sin entered the world, suffering entered the world also, and it has been around ever since.

All suffering is the result of sin on some level. But suffering is not necessarily caused by personal sin. We live in a world filled with sin, and it affects all of us at various times. Jesus is our Healer and our Deliverer, and if He doesn't take away our suffering while we are on earth, it will definitely be gone when we go to heaven. Once we get there, all pain, suffering, and crying will have ceased (Revelation 21:4).

I couldn't and wouldn't even try to answer all the questions people have about why children are starving in some parts of the world or why a child suffers with cancer. I can't explain why mean people sometimes live long lives, while some good people die young. I just know that God is good, and He hates suffering and pain as much as we do.

There are times when suffering drives a person to God when they would never accept Him otherwise. In these cases, we can easily see the good that comes from the pain. I love this quote from C. S. Lewis:

> We...will admit that we can ignore even pleasure. But pain insists upon being attended to. God whispers to us in our pleasures, speaks in our conscience, but shouts in our pain: it is His megaphone to rouse a deaf world. . . .
>
> No doubt Pain as God's megaphone is a terrible instrument; it may lead to final and unrepented rebellion. But it gives the only opportunity the bad man can have for amendment. It removes the veil; it plants the flag of truth within the fortress of the rebel soul.[28]

We don't tend to be too curious about the suffering that comes to people we may not view as "good people," but when bad things happen to those we do see as being good people, our minds are filled with questions. I don't know all the answers, but I do know God is a just God, and He makes all wrong things right in His timing. When we go through trials, difficulties, pain, and suffering, if we handle ourselves the way God wants us to, He will bring a double portion (blessing) into our lives (Isaiah 61:7).

Our Chaotic World

The world we live in today is often chaotic. Crime rates are up, suicides are up, and for most people stress is at an all-time high. Our world is changing so fast that we sometimes feel we can barely keep up with it. The Bible says that, in the last days, conditions in the world will be so bad that people's hearts will fail them due to fear (Luke 21:26 NKJV).

Being able to trust God and not live in fear is wonderful. It gives us peace in the midst of life's storms. The peace God gives is a peace that the world cannot understand because it is not based on having to have all the answers. It is based on knowing God, who does have all the answers.

What to Do Spiritually When You Don't Have Practical Answers for Your Problems

What should we do when we don't know how to solve our problems? The Bible gives us this advice:

- Study God's Word, because it is a lamp to your feet and a light to your path (Psalm 119:105).
- Psalm 37:3 tells us to trust God and keep doing what is good.
- Ephesians 6:13 (AMPC) tells us to "put on God's complete armor," resist the devil, and stand our ground "on the evil day [of danger], and, having done all [the crisis demands], to stand [firmly in your place]." Do what you can do, but don't try to do what you cannot do.
- "Be thankful and say so to Him" (Psalm 100:4 AMPC).
- Jesus told His disciples "that they should always pray and not give up" (Luke 18:1), and so should we.

And here is some practical advice:

- Don't pay too much attention to the bad reports you hear.
- Do what you would do if you didn't have a problem.
- Keep your commitments.
- Keep giving and being a blessing to others.
- Keep declaring God's Word, rather than talking about your circumstances.

Finally, don't forget to enjoy your life. People tend to think they cannot enjoy life as long as they have a problem, but this is not true. "The joy of the Lord is your strength" (Nehemiah 8:10), and "a merry heart does good, like medicine" (Proverbs 17:22 NKJV). Remaining joyful during life's trials will confuse the enemy, and your victory will come much sooner than it would if you were depressed and sad. Let's not forget what Jesus says: "In this world you will have trouble. But take heart! I have overcome the world" (John 16:33).

CHAPTER 14

Be Confident That You Always Triumph in Christ

When we pray for the Spirit's help...we will simply fall down at the Lord's feet in our weakness. There we will find the victory and power that comes from His love.

Andrew Murray[29]

When we feel like our lives are in a mess, we can be tempted to think the whole world is against us. But the truth is that we are destined to triumph over opposition. Our inheritance as believers in Christ is to be winners and victors in life. Isaiah 54:17 says, "This [peace, righteousness, security, triumph over opposition] is the heritage of the servants of the Lord" (AMPC), meaning our inheritance from Him.

The way we handle opposition is very important. We win when the devil does his worst and we come out of our trouble still loving God and loving people, with our faith even stronger than it was before the opposition came against us. This hope of victory during our tests and tribulations is extremely important. Hope empowers us to keep going even when we feel we cannot go on. What we focus on is a key to our triumph. If we focus on our problems too much, they will overwhelm us. Hebrews 12:2 (AMPC) tells us to look away "[from all that will distract] to Jesus, Who is the Leader and the Source of our faith . . . and is also its Finisher."

When facing difficulties and opposition, we should remember past victories and remind ourselves that all things are possible with God (Matthew 19:26). Let's think and talk about what God can do, not what the devil has done.

Think and talk about what God can do, not what the devil has done.

Problems are difficult, but triumph is sweet. Second Corinthians 2:14 tells us that Christ *always* leads us in triumph: "But thanks be to God, Who in Christ always leads us in triumph [as trophies of Christ's victory] and through us spreads and makes evident the fragrance of the knowledge of God everywhere" (AMPC).

I was born in 1943, so I have been alive for quite a while. During those years, I have faced my fair share of difficult problems, but my testimony is "I'm still here." I am still loving Jesus and still helping people. I have experienced God's faithfulness more times than I can count, and I am full of faith for the future. At the time of the publication of this book, I am eighty years young. I say that because age is a number, while "old" is a mindset. When I tell you my age, you may think, *She is really old*. But I don't feel that way at all. I feel young at heart, and I believe I have a lot of experience God can use to help other people.

In my life, I have overcome sexual, mental, and emotional abuse; a bad marriage with a cheating husband when I was young (before I met Dave); a miscarriage; two hip replacements; breast cancer; betrayal; unjust treatment; being lied about; being disappointed by people I trusted; being stolen from; and many other things. Besides these, I have dealt with the daily pressures we all deal with. However, my faith is stronger now than it has ever been. I have victory, I have triumphed in life, and I am more than a conqueror through Christ (Romans 8:37). I have experienced God's faithfulness over and over again, and you will also if you put your trust in Him.

No matter what has happened to you, don't let yourself develop a victim mentality. If you see yourself as a victim, that's what you will always be. We do go through difficult things in life, but they are nothing compared to what Jesus went through for us. His story ends in victory, and so will ours. Paul said he could be content whether he was in need or had plenty (Philippians 4:12). He also said he could do all things through Christ who was his strength (Philippians 4:13), and we can too.

> No matter what, don't let yourself develop a victim mentality.

In and through Christ

Our victory is not of ourselves. It doesn't come from our will-power. It is in and through Christ and His love. As long as we remember that He loves us, no matter what we are going through, we will remain strong. When we have trouble, we are wise to turn to God for help immediately, because our problems will be solved only in and through Him. God is called "an ever-present help in trouble" (Psalm 46:1) and His Holy Spirit is our Helper (John 14:16–17).

> God is our refuge and strength, an ever-present help in trouble. Therefore we will not fear, though the earth give way and the mountains fall into the heart of the sea, though its waters roar and foam and the mountains quake with their surging.
>
> Psalm 46:1–3

The apostle Paul faced many difficulties, yet he was victorious over each one. His pain was real, but he trusted that God had a purpose in all things. He felt that some of the difficulties he went through encouraged other believers to be bold in sharing the good news of the gospel and to be strong as they faced their own tests and trials.

Paul was beaten many times, jailed, went hungry, spent a day and night on the open sea, labored and toiled for the sake of the gospel, and often went without sleep. He also said he had been cold and naked (2 Corinthians 11:24–27). In 2 Corinthians 4:17–18 (ESV), he refers to these as light afflictions:

> For this light momentary affliction is preparing for us an eternal weight of glory beyond all comparison, as we look

not to the things that are seen but to the things that are unseen. For the things that are seen are transient, but the things that are unseen are eternal.

Paul looked forward to eternity much more than he looked at his problems. Perhaps we are not eternity-minded enough. Even if we lived one hundred years on earth, it would be nothing compared to eternity.

We will never understand all the reasons for our trials, but I do know that one reason for them is to keep us from trusting in ourselves and to teach us to trust God. Some people will never trust God until He is all they have left to lean on.

> Some people will never trust God until He is all they have left.

I hear people say, and I have said myself, "Well, Lord, I guess there is nothing left to do but pray." This, of course, is a foolish statement, because praying should be our first course of action, not the last resort after we have tried everything else.

I don't know what you may be going through right now, but I do know that you will triumph in Christ if you handle the opposition the way God wants you to.

The wife of one of my friends died of cancer, even though thousands of people had prayed for her healing. The first thing he said to the Lord was "Lord, please help me do this right." This friend is a pastor, and I was deeply touched that his main concern was that he would handle the loss of his wife in a way that would glorify God as he continued to minister to others.

My friend could have been bitter and said, "Lord, I have served You all these years and have seen many others healed. I have prayed for people, preached to them, and helped them through their difficulties, and when I needed a miracle, You let me down." He could have said that, but he didn't. Instead, he told God, "I will never ask You why." He wanted God to know that he trusted Him enough that he didn't need to know why. I'm not saying it is wrong to ask why, but when we do, we may not get an answer, and we need to be okay with that. There are many mysteries hidden in God, and at times, we will have to trust in His goodness in the midst of our confusion and pain.

We Are More Than Conquerors

Consider these powerful words from Romans 8:35–39:

> Who shall separate us from the love of Christ? Shall trouble or hardship or persecution or famine or nakedness or danger or sword? As it is written: "For your sake we face death all day long; we are considered as sheep to be slaughtered." No, in all these things we are more than conquerors through him who loved us. For I am convinced that neither death nor life, neither angels nor demons, neither the present nor the future, nor any powers, neither height nor depth, nor anything else in all creation, will be able to separate us from the love of God that is in Christ Jesus our Lord.

This Scripture passage shows us that it is important for us not to let anything separate us from the love of God that is in Christ Jesus. We should be so certain that God loves us that we refuse to allow any kind of trouble to come between us and His love.

Never allow any kind of trouble to come between you and God's love.

What does it mean to be more than a conqueror? I think it means that we know we have victory in life even before we have a problem. A victorious mindset enables us to live without fear of trouble. I remember times in my life when I dreaded having any kind of a problem because I knew it would cause me to be afraid, and I would worry about it until it was solved. Now I simply deal with things as they come, and I am assured that God will take care of them in His timing and in His own way. This is what makes us more than conquerors. If we believe that God loves us, we can also believe He will always do what is best for us. His love makes us secure and gives us confidence.

> Believing God loves you means believing He will do what is best for you.

There are many scriptures that tell us God will give us victory, including Deuteronomy 20:4, "For the Lord your God is the one who goes with you to fight for you against your enemies to give you victory," and Romans 8:31, "If God is for us, who can be against us?"

God's Timing and His Ways

God's ways are not our ways, and His timing is not always what we think it should be. At times, God's ways are surprising. We expect Him to do one thing, and He does something totally different. His timing is perfect in our lives, and we should be content to rest in

> Your positive words are darts thrown against Satan.

Him until He causes us to triumph over our trials. Because He has promised that He will cause us to triumph (2 Corinthians 2:14), why would we be concerned about how and when?

While you are waiting for your victory, there are some things you can say that will help you stay encouraged, and your positive words will be darts thrown against Satan. You can make statements such as:

- "This will end well!"
- "In all things God works for the good of those who love him, who have been called according to his purpose" (Romans 8:28).
- "God is working on my problem right now."
- "I know that God loves me."
- "God, I trust You!"

Of course, Satan wants us to be filled with doubt and to make negative comments, but positive speech that is based on God's Word will help defeat him.

God would prefer that you not make comments such as:

- "I'm afraid God won't come through in time."
- "I feel like God doesn't love me."
- "It seems like I have one trial after another. I wonder what I'm doing wrong."
- "Maybe God is punishing me for the sins of my past."
- "I may as well give up, because nothing good ever happens to me."

None of these statements agree with God's Word, so saying them is counterproductive.

I hope you can see what a difference it will make if you stay positive, believing you will triumph over whatever you are going through.

Trust God for Favor

One of the blessings God gives us is His favor. This means that people will want to do things for us and not understand why they are inclined to be good to us or that situations will work out well for us and we will not even know why. We experience God's favor when we apply for jobs and employers choose us, or when clerks in stores give us discounts on our purchases when we didn't even know such discounts were available. Favor is an amazing thing, and it is also a lot of fun to experience and receive when God gives it to you.

Experiencing God's favor is one way you can be blessed in your mess. Ask God for favor and release your faith for it. Everything we receive from God comes through faith. Faith is a powerful force that abides in your spirit, but it needs to be released in order for it to do any good. We can release our faith by praying, speaking in agreement with God's Word, and taking God-inspired actions.

If the idea of God's favor is new to you and you have never asked for it, you are missing a tremendous blessing that God wants you to enjoy. Just look at these scriptures about favor:

> Let the favor of the Lord our God be upon us, and establish the work of our hands upon us; yes, establish the work of our hands!
>
> Psalm 90:17 ESV

> Now the boy Samuel continued to grow both in stature and in favor with the Lord and also with man.
>
> 1 Samuel 2:26 ESV

> And the Lord said to Moses, "This very thing that you have spoken I will do, for you have found favor in my sight, and I know you by name."
>
> Exodus 33:17 ESV

Noah had favor with God (Genesis 6:8), and David had favor with God (Acts 7:45–46). Esther had favor with the king of Persia

(Esther 2:17). Ruth had favor with Boaz (Ruth 2:10–13). Joseph had favor with Potiphar, the jailer, and Pharaoh (Genesis 39:4, 21; 41:39–44). Many other people mentioned in the Bible also experienced favor.

In the New Testament, we learn that we are saved by grace (Ephesians 2:8), and I define *grace* in part as "God's undeserved favor." Mary, the mother of Jesus, found favor with God (Luke 1:30), and even Jesus grew in stature and favor with God and man (Luke 2:52).

Each day when you pray, ask God for favor, and you will begin to see some marvelous things happen in your life. Remember that favor is not something you earn; otherwise, it would not be favor.

Repent and boldly ask God for favor.

Favor is undeserved, so don't be shy about asking for it even if you have made mistakes. Just repent and boldly ask God for favor.

CHAPTER 15

Just Ask

You pay God a great compliment by asking great things of Him.

Teresa of Avila[30]

There is a wonderful lesson to be learned from James 4:1–2:

> What causes fights and quarrels among you? Don't they come from your desires that battle within you? You desire but do not have, so you kill. You covet but you cannot get what you want, so you quarrel and fight. You do not have because you do not ask God.

God gave me insight into these verses at a time in my life when I was extremely frustrated because I was trying to get some things I wanted, and nothing I did was working. They were not bad things. For example, I wanted my ministry to grow. I wanted to change and be more like I thought Jesus wanted me to be. I wanted other people to change and be easier for me to get along with. I wanted and wanted and wanted, but I had failed to simply ask God for what I wanted. Perhaps sometimes we think we can ask God to forgive us for the bad things we do but fail to realize we can and should also ask Him for the good things we want.

The worst thing that can happen if we ask God for something that isn't His will for us is that He won't give it to us. But He won't be angry with us for asking. James goes on to say that sometimes we do not receive because our motives for asking are wrong (James 4:3). We are asking selfishly, thinking only of ourselves. If this is the case, the Holy Spirit will correct us and teach us how to pray accurately.

Maybe you are not asking God for big enough things.

Ephesians 3:20 says that God can do much more than we could ever think, hope, or imagine. Maybe you are not asking God for big enough things. I often say I would rather ask God for a lot and get some of it than to ask Him for nothing and get all of it.

There are material blessings and spiritual blessings, and the spiritual ones are most important. Ephesians 1:3 says: "Blessed be the God and Father of our Lord Jesus Christ, who *has blessed us in Christ with every spiritual blessing* in the heavenly places" (ESV, emphasis mine).

God has *already* provided every spiritual blessing in Christ, and He is simply waiting for us to ask to receive them. We can ask God to help us be more like Jesus, to help us grow spiritually, and to enable us to bring glory to Him in all we do. Ask Him to bring across your path people in need so you can help them. Ask Him for opportunities to share your faith with people who don't know Jesus. There are countless spiritual blessings we can and should ask for, in addition to the material things we need and want.

> God is waiting for you to ask for every spiritual blessing He has already provided.

Don't be afraid to ask God for big things, because He is a big God who loves to do big things. Always remember that He wants to bless you not because you are good but because *He* is good.

If you need a new car, you can ask God for one. If you have never owned your own home and owning a place to live is a desire of your heart, you can ask Him to bring it about. If we delight ourselves in the Lord, He will give us the desires of our heart (Psalm 37:4).

God Is a Giving God

One of the greatest verses in the Bible is John 3:16: "For God so loved the world that he gave his one and only Son, that whoever believes in him shall not perish but have eternal life." In giving Jesus, God gave His best and His only. If you have children, then you know what it's like to love someone and want to do things for them, especially when they need help. It would make me sad if my children had needs and felt they could not come to Dave and me and ask for help. When you love your family, their problems become your problems also.

Occasionally, one of our children may ask for something to which we have to say no. But we only say no if we cannot help or if we don't feel it would be best for them at the time, and they respect our decisions. We should be the same way with the Lord. Ask Him for anything, and be content with what He gives you, knowing that He always does what is best for you.

Philippians 4:19 says, "And my God will supply every need of yours according to his riches in glory in Christ Jesus" (ESV).

One of my daughters recently commented that she loved a piece of my jewelry, and immediately I wanted to give it to her. Nothing blesses me more than blessing my children. If I feel that way, I can only imagine how much God delights in blessing His children who love Him. I really want you to believe that God loves to bless you, and I want you to have the freedom and boldness to ask Him for anything.

> *Have the freedom and boldness to ask God for anything.*

I will never forget a clerk I met in a department store. I discovered through conversation that she had been a Christian for more than thirty years. As we talked, I asked her if she worked strictly on commission or was a salaried employee. She said that she got a salary but had to meet certain quotas in order to keep her job. She was concerned because she had not been meeting those quotas recently.

I said, "Well, do you ask God to give customers a desire to come to your section so you can wait on them?"

She looked at me with a puzzled expression and asked, "Would it be okay for me to ask God to help me with something concerning money?"

Of course, I told her that it would be okay and that God would be delighted to help her.

It made me sad that this woman had been in church for more than thirty years and didn't know that God is generous and wants to help us with all our needs, including needs involving money. She had a need, and God wants to meet all of our needs according to His riches in glory in Christ Jesus (Philippians 4:19).

You have not because you ask not (James 4:2). Start asking God for big things and see what He will do for you. If the timing isn't right for you to have what you ask for, then you will need to wait for it, but you can still ask.

> Start asking God for big things.

I Don't Deserve That!

The reasons people are reluctant to ask God for big things are interesting to me. I was hesitant to ask for big things until God taught me better. I believe that many times we don't ask because we know we don't deserve any of God's blessings, let alone big ones. We ask if we are desperate for God's help, but if it is something "extra" that we could do without, we are often not bold enough to ask for it. I think God wants to do more for us than we even know how to ask for. Do you know that God wants you to approach His throne boldly? Hebrews 4:15–16 (AMPC) says:

> For we do not have a High Priest Who is unable to understand and sympathize and have a shared feeling with our weaknesses and infirmities and liability to the assaults

of temptation, but One Who has been tempted in every respect as we are, yet without sinning.

Let us then fearlessly and confidently and boldly draw near to the throne of grace (the throne of God's unmerited favor to us sinners), that we may receive mercy [for our failures] and find grace to help in good time for every need [appropriate help and well-timed help, coming just when we need it].

Because we know that God loves us, we can go boldly to His throne and ask for whatever we need, even when we know we are far from perfect in our behavior. We all have weaknesses, but weakness is different from wickedness. God looks at the heart. Many people who have a heart after God also have weaknesses they are working through, and those weaknesses won't keep God from helping and blessing them.

Jesus told His disciples that they were clean already because of the Word He had given them (John 15:3). This scripture once confused me because I thought, *How can they be clean?* Peter was going to deny Him (Luke 22:34), and they argued among themselves about which of them was the greatest (Luke 22:24). Thomas was negative and often filled with doubt (John 20:24–29).

So, again, how could they be clean? I understood this when I realized that weaknesses are different from wickedness. They had weakness, but they loved Jesus and were not wicked. Thankfully, God sees our heart. Jesus understands our weaknesses, and if we will go boldly to the throne and ask for His help, we will find mercy, not judgment (Hebrews 4:16).

> You don't always get what you deserve, but you share in what Jesus deserves.

We all make mistakes. We sin and truly don't deserve God's help in any area of life. Thankfully, we don't get what we deserve, but we share in what Jesus deserves. We are co-heirs with Jesus (Romans 8:17). Here is an example to demonstrate what it means to be an heir with Christ: Dave and I have a will so that when God calls us home to heaven, our children will all get an equal share of whatever we have. And I know their children will get a share of what they receive from us. Neither our children nor our grandchildren will have worked for what we will leave to them. Dave and I have done the work, and they will inherit what we have worked for and earned. This is based totally on our relationship with them and nothing else. We love them and we know they love us.

God knows we could not ever deserve His goodness, and this is one reason He sent Jesus. Jesus had no sin, and He deserves everything God has. If we believe in Him and have a good relationship with Him, loving Him with all of our heart, then we can join Him in enjoying His inheritance. What He has becomes ours.

Never forget that God's Word says that we do not have because we do not ask. When we do ask, we must ask in faith, and faith must be released in order for it to work. One way it is released is through praying (asking).

I really like what Ephesians 3:12 says: "In Whom, because of our faith in Him, we dare to have the boldness (courage and confidence) of free access (an unreserved approach to God with freedom and without fear)" (AMPC). Just imagine, because of Jesus and our faith in Him, we can daringly have the boldness to come before God anytime, knowing we are welcome. He tells us to approach Him with confidence and boldness.

Consider also 1 John 5:14: "And this is the confidence (the assurance, the privilege of boldness) which we have in Him: [we are sure] that if we ask anything (make any request) according to His will (in agreement with His own plan), He listens to and hears us" (AMPC). How do you approach God in prayer? Do you go to Him boldly, expecting Him to answer, or do you approach Him with hesitation, wondering if it is all right for you to ask for what you need and want? To go boldly doesn't mean to come without reverence. We always approach God with reverence, respect, and awe, but we don't have to approach Him in fear or apprehension.

Ask God to Turn Your Trouble into a Blessing

Take a step of faith and ask God to take your trouble (mess) and make it a blessing. Ask Him for the double portion we read about in Isaiah 61:7. Even if you know that part of your mess was caused by your own lack of wisdom or sin, you can repent and still ask God to work it out for your good (Romans 8:28).

You can be radically and outrageously blessed if you are bold enough to ask for such blessings. I know you may be thinking, *But I don't deserve it!* This is true, and it is one reason God's blessings are so good. We don't deserve them, but Jesus took our place, paid for our sin, took our punishment, and has arranged a good life for us to live. Just remember that you have not because you ask not. The Bible says, "Ask, and you will receive, that your joy may be full" (John 16:24 NKJV). This is good news! Ask, ask, and then ask some more. If you ask for nothing, that's what you will get. But if you are bold enough to ask for great things, you can get ready to be amazed.

There are two parts to God's promises to bless us. There is God's part, and we know He will always be faithful to do what He has said He will do. Then, there is our part. As I mentioned in a previous chapter, if we expect radical and outrageous blessings, we should give God radical and outrageous obedience.

> *If you expect outrageous blessings, you should give God outrageous obedience.*

With this in mind, make sure you faithfully do three simple things. I believe these things represent the areas in which most people fail to be obedient and consequently forfeit the outrageous blessings God wants to give them:

1. When you sin, repent immediately and sincerely.
2. Don't allow unforgiveness toward anyone to remain in your heart, because unforgiveness hinders prayer.
3. Be extremely thankful for all God has done and continually does for you. God will answer prayers, but He doesn't answer complaints. Gratitude prevents us from complaining.

In addition to these three, I try to be careful to keep my heart free of offense, because I would rather be blessed than angry, and hopefully you would too. This may be challenging at times, but we always have the power of the Holy Spirit available to us to help us do the hard things God asks us to do.

Again, keep in mind that you have not if you don't ask. Start asking God for anything you need and want, and keep on asking. I know I have repeated this several times, but I have done so on purpose because it is difficult for us to believe it's true. Just make sure your petitions don't outweigh your praise to God. Love God, obey Him, enjoy the blessings you have, and look forward to the ones that are on their way to you right now. God will meet your needs. He will give you what you want if it is right for you, and He will do it at the right time.

Psalm 37:4 says that if we delight ourselves in the Lord, He will give us the desires of our heart. This scripture excites me. We don't have to chase things. Instead, we can chase God, and the things that are right for us will be given at the proper time.

CHAPTER 16

How to Be Blessed and Have Less of a Mess

All these blessings will come on you and accompany you if you obey the Lord your God.

Deuteronomy 28:2

According to Ecclesiastes 12:13 in the Amplified Bible, Classic Edition, honoring God is the basis for happiness and "the adjustment to all inharmonious circumstances":

> All has been heard; the end of the matter is: Fear God [revere and worship Him, knowing that He is] and keep His commandments, for this is the whole of man [the full, original purpose of his creation, the object of God's providence, the root of character, the foundation of all happiness, the adjustment to all inharmonious circumstances and conditions under the sun] and the whole [duty] for every man.

Solomon penned this verse of Scripture, and I think it is marvelous. Solomon tried everything imaginable to make himself happy. He denied himself no pleasure and owned everything a person could want. He built houses and had multiple wives and concubines, but no matter what he had, he was never satisfied. He said that everything was vanity. It was useless, like "chasing after the wind" (Ecclesiastes 1:14).

Ecclesiastes 12:13 comes from the last chapter of the Book of Ecclesiastes, and at that point Solomon had finally found the answer to his quest for happiness: to revere and worship God and keep His commandments. This, according to Solomon, is "the full, original purpose of his creation" and "the whole [duty] for every man" (AMPC). He goes on to say in this verse that honoring God is "the foundation of all happiness" and the only thing that will fix circumstances and conditions that make us unhappy.

This is quite a statement, and I think it sums up the answer to all our questions.

How can you be blessed and have less of a mess? Just follow the guidelines in Ecclesiastes 12:13, and little by little your mess will turn into a life of blessing.

The Amplified Bible, Classic Edition indicates that *blessed* means "happy, to be envied, and spiritually prosperous—with life-joy and satisfaction in God's favor and salvation, regardless of their outward conditions" (Matthew 5:3).

As I mentioned earlier, true prosperity is not only about having money and material possessions. God does want us to have our needs met and to be able to give to others, but true prosperity encompasses success in every area of life. Of all the various ways people can prosper, spiritual prosperity is the most important.

The Hebrew word for *prosper, tsalach,* means "to succeed, prosper." It "generally expresses the idea of a successful venture, versus failure" and is "sometimes used in such a way as to indicate victory."[31] The New Testament word for *prosper, euodoo,* means "to help on one's way."[32]

What Do We Really Want?

People often mistakenly think they want material things, or they want their circumstances to change, but what we really want is to be at peace, to have joy, to feel well and strong physically, to have people who love us, and to have someone to love. I also think we all want to believe we are making a difference in the world. We want to put our time into something that has value. I believe the key to the fulfillment of all of these desires is to live in obedience to God.

Let's think about relationships, for example: If we use good manners and basic courtesies, such as saying "please" and "thank you," we help keep our relationships pleasant. If we are unselfish, kind, and encouraging, and we apologize when we are wrong and don't argue over frivolous things, we go a long way toward keeping our relationships healthy. God's Word teaches us all we need to know about having good relationships.

God's Word is practical, and we can easily apply its teachings to our circumstances—especially teachings from Proverbs, Psalms, and the New Testament.

One theme that repeats itself throughout the Old Testament is that when the Israelites obeyed God, they were blessed, they had favor, and they won their wars. But when they forgot God and walked in their own ways, they were not blessed. As we read the Old Testament, this scenario takes place so many times under so many circumstances that I don't see how anyone could miss it.

The same principle is true today. When we obey God, we are blessed; and when we don't obey Him, we miss out on His blessings. We don't earn God's blessings with our good works, but we are rewarded for the good we do from a heart made pure by Jesus. No matter how well we behave, we can never deserve God's goodness. But if our heart is right before Him and we seek to please Him, He is pleased.

> If you don't obey God, you miss out on His blessings.

Hebrews 11:6 teaches us: "Without faith it is impossible to please God, because anyone who comes to him must believe that he exists and that he rewards those who earnestly seek him." Are you earnestly seeking God? If so, you probably won't behave perfectly (because no one does)—you will either walk in obedience to God or be repentant when you don't. You will not be able to live a sloppy, sinful life and not care.

Radical Obedience and Outrageous Blessings

There are times when God asks us to obey Him in ways that may seem radical. If we do, there will be an outrageous blessing coming our way. Our God is a big God, and He delights in doing big things for His children. For example, if we obey God in our giving, He will open the windows of heaven and pour out blessings so great we cannot contain them (Malachi 3:10). He doesn't promise to dribble out blessings, but to pour them out in such abundance that we are totally amazed. No matter how many problems we have, we have many reasons to thank God for His goodness in our lives. Being aggressively thankful is one of the keys to living and enjoying a blessed life.

> God may ask you to obey Him in ways that seem radical.

According to 1 Corinthians 2:9 (AMPC), God has many good things stored up for us:

> But, on the contrary, as the Scripture says, What eye has not seen and ear has not heard and has not entered into the heart of man, [all that] God has prepared (made and keeps ready) for those who love Him [who hold Him in affectionate reverence, promptly obeying Him and gratefully recognizing the benefits He has bestowed].

This scripture clearly tells us that what God has stored up for His children is beyond anything we have ever seen or heard of, and it is made ready for those who promptly obey Him and are thankful for all He has done and is doing.

God is able to do "exceedingly abundantly above" and beyond all that we could ever dare to hope, ask, or think (Ephesians 3:20

NKJV). In Psalm 23:5, David notes that God even prepared a table before him in the presence of his enemies.

Not only does God want to give to us, but He also wants us to be generous in giving to others. Luke 6:38 (AMPC) makes a great promise to those who give:

> Give, and [gifts] will be given to you; good measure, pressed down, shaken together, and running over, will they pour into [the pouch formed by] the bosom [of your robe and used as a bag]. For with the measure you deal out [with the measure you use when you confer benefits on others], it will be measured back to you.

You may say, "Joyce, I have been giving, and I haven't seen the kind of blessing this scripture promises." Let me ask: Are you just giving what is easy for you to give or what you feel like giving, or are you giving all that God asks you to give? Only you know the answer to this question. God has a timing for all things He has planned in our life, and it is important for us to *continue* in our obedience to Him no matter how long it takes for His blessings to come to pass. In regard to giving, for example, perhaps the thing for you to do is to keep on giving. Again, only you know the details of your specific situation, but sometimes God is looking for perseverance.

We see the word *continue* often in the Bible, and it is an important word. *To continue* means to keep doing something until you get a desired result and then still keep doing it. We can't do the right thing once and expect the windows of heaven to open for us. Jesus says that if we "continue in" His Word (John 8:31 KJV), we will know the truth and it will make us free (John 8:32). We are told to continue in God's love (John 15:9 KJV). Paul and Barnabas encouraged the believers in the early church to "continue in the grace of God" (Acts 13:43 NKJV) and exhorted the early disciples to "continue in the faith" (Acts 14:22 NKJV). We read in Colossians 4:2 (NKJV) that we are to "continue earnestly in prayer." Paul urged Timothy to "continue in the things which you have learned" regarding faith (2 Timothy 3:14 NKJV). And Hebrews 13:1 says, "Let brotherly love continue" (NKJV).

Being a Christian is not something we practice once a week on Sunday morning; it is a lifestyle. We continue doing what God's Word teaches. Early followers of Jesus referred to their Christian faith as

> *Being a Christian is a lifestyle, not something you practice once a week on Sunday.*

"The Way" because it was the way people were instructed to live.

Radical Obedience

I know many people who have obeyed God in radical ways, and perhaps you do too. When I say that people obeyed God "in radical ways," I mean they followed God into something that was beyond normal day-to-day obedience. God asked them to do something that made no sense to their minds, and I'm sure that in most instances they did not feel like doing it.

I will give you a few practical examples from my life. God asked me to take care of my parents, who had abused me, and to make sure they had a good life. God asked me to give away my favorite coat to a woman who had hurt me badly. He guided me to quit my job when it meant Dave and I would need a miracle every month just to pay our bills. He asked me to leave

> *Radical obedience is God's way of teaching you to trust Him.*

my job at the church where I was an associate pastor and take my teaching ministry north, south, east, and west. This may sound exciting, but in those days, nobody knew who I was. I live in Saint Louis, Missouri, so I started teaching a monthly Bible meeting in North St. Louis, South St. Louis, East St. Louis, and West St. Louis. That was all I knew to do. Gradually, from there, our ministry has spread around the world. Anyone God is going to use will have to take steps of faith that will not always make sense to the natural mind and that will take us out of our comfort zone. Part of the reason God asks us to take steps of radical obedience is that He is testing our level of commitment to Him and teaching us to trust Him.

Biblical Men and Women Who Radically Obeyed God

The Bible is full of stories of radical obedience. Let's consider a few of them.

Noah Built the Ark

In Genesis 6:13, God told Noah He would destroy the earth and all the people in it because of sin. He went on to tell Noah to build an ark (a huge boat) so he and his family would survive the devastating flood that would cover the earth. He gave Noah the exact specifications of the ark and told him to take two of all the living creatures (a male and a female) so they could begin to repopulate the earth after the flood.

Although Noah had never seen a flood and had no visible signs that what God told him was true, he obeyed God and built the ark. Hebrews 11:7 says: "By faith Noah, when warned about things not yet seen, in holy fear built an ark to save his family." Just imagine how foolish people thought he was. I am sure he himself wondered at times if he was really hearing from God.

Scholars don't agree about how many years it took for Noah to build the ark. Some say twenty to forty years, while others say it took 120 years, to allow people living in those days ample time to repent for their sinful ways. Whether it took twenty years or 120 years, Noah had a long time to think about what he was doing. I am sure the devil told Noah he was crazy, but he obeyed God and was blessed, because only he and his family survived the flood. God asked Noah to do something radical, and he obeyed, not allowing his own mind or the opinions of other people to stop him. Has God asked you to do something that seems radical to you? If so, are you following the Holy Spirit in radical obedience, or are you letting your reasoning guide you?

Daniel Stayed Loyal to God

Daniel was a young Jewish man who was captured and taken from his home in Jerusalem to serve in the court of King Darius in Babylon. In Babylon, he was surrounded by people who did not follow God and did not respect his religion. Yet he was promoted above all those working around him. This happened because Daniel's "exceptional qualities" (Daniel 6:3) distinguished him among the administrators of the court to the degree that the king put him in charge of the entire realm (Daniel 6:1–4). Daniel was a man of excellence (Daniel 5:12) and obedience to God. Because Daniel had favor with the king, some of the jealous people around him asked the king to make a law stating that for thirty days no one could pray to any god or human being except the king. The penalty for breaking this law was being thrown into a den of lions (Daniel 6:7). They knew Daniel wouldn't obey that law and hoped to see him killed. Daniel continued praying, as he had always done, and got on his knees with the windows open and prayed to God three times a day (Daniel 6:10). Because of this, he did end up being thrown into the lions' den (Daniel 6:16). King Darius liked Daniel, but had to obey his own decree, so when Daniel was thrown into the lions' den, the king said to him, "May your God, whom you serve continually, rescue you!" (Daniel 6:16). God sent an angel to shut the lions' mouths, and Daniel came out unharmed (Daniel 6:22).

Throughout his captivity, Daniel refused to compromise, and God protected and blessed him.

Abram Left Everything Familiar

Abram (later called Abraham) was told to leave his father's house and everything he knew and go to a place God would show him (Genesis 12:1). But God would not tell him where He was leading him until after he started his journey. This sounds fairly radical to me. Had it happened to me, I might have obeyed, but I'm pretty sure I would have at least wanted to know where I was going.

God promised Abram that He would bless him and make his name great and make him a blessing (Genesis 12:2). He said that all those who blessed him would be blessed, and that all the people on the earth would be blessed through him (Genesis 12:3). Yet Abram didn't have even one child, and he was too old to have one with Sarah, his wife, without a miracle (Genesis 18:11). But Abram believed God, and God credited that to him as righteousness (Genesis 15:6). When Abram was ninety-nine years old, God appeared to him, and Abram fell on his face before Him (Genesis 17:1–3). God changed his name to Abraham, saying, "I have made you a father of many nations" (Genesis 17:5).

Others Who Were Radically Obedient to God

God's Word tells the stories of many other people who obeyed God radically. In the Old Testament, we read about people such as Ruth, who remained faithful to her mother-in-law, Naomi, even though it meant leaving her homeland (Ruth 1:15–19), and eventually married a very wealthy, well-respected man (Ruth 4:13). We also read the story of Esther, a young Jewish woman who risked approaching the king without being invited (a breach of protocol) and ultimately saved her nation (Esther 4:12–14; 8:1–8). In addition, we see the story of Joseph, who, although his brothers mistreated him severely, (Genesis 37:4–28), was given favor with God and man (Genesis 39:20–23). He went to prison for years for something he did not do (Genesis 39:6–20), but he eventually ended up in the palace second only to Pharaoh (Genesis 41:41-43).

In the New Testament, we read about the disciples who walked away from their businesses and followed Jesus (Matthew 4:18–22). And Jesus Himself was extremely obedient, even unto death. Paul writes about this in Philippians 2:8–10 (AMPC):

> And after He had appeared in human form, He abased and humbled Himself [still further] and carried His obedience to the extreme of death, even the death of the cross! Therefore [because He stooped so low] God has highly exalted Him and has freely bestowed on Him the name that is above every name, that in (at) the name of Jesus every knee should (must) bow, in heaven and on earth and under the earth.

If God outrageously blessed the people we read about in Scripture for their radical obedience, we can expect Him to do the same for us, because He "does not show favoritism" (Romans 2:11). I think one of our problems is that we often read the Bible without taking it to heart personally. We read it as though we are reading other people's stories, which of course we are, but God wants to do for us what He has done for the people we read about.

As I mentioned previously, when I began my relationship with God through Jesus, my entire life was a mess. I truly cannot think of any area in which I did not have a problem. I went to church for several years and saw no changes. I desperately wanted my circumstances to change, but I finally learned that I had to let God change *me* before my life would change.

> I had to let God change me before my life would change.

I started learning how to be obedient to God, but it was a process. First, I had to study God's Word and realize that it was so much more than an ancient book written to a group of people who were no longer alive, but also written to me. Even though the world has been modernized since the writing of the Scriptures, God's moral law is still the same. I had to learn that if I wanted my life to change and be blessed, I had to learn how to be obedient— sometimes radically obedient—to God.

God asked me to do some things that made no sense to me. They didn't seem fair, and I didn't want to do them. But because I loved the Lord, I did do them, and I was blessed for doing so.

> If you will be radically obedient to God, you will have less of a mess in your life.

One time I fasted for thirty days. Although my pastor did not know I had been fasting or that I had just finished, he called me into his office and said that God had put it on his heart to ordain me into ministry and make me an associate pastor at the church. I was thrilled more than I know how to express. It was as though God was saying, "I have called you and I am honoring you."

If you will be radically obedient to God, you will eventually have less of a mess in your life. As you continue in obedience, the mess will become smaller and smaller. Eventually God's blessings will overtake you and the messy way you once lived will become a distant memory. If you feel you have a long, long way to go, don't be discouraged. Every day you make progress takes you one more day closer to living the blessed life God wants you to have. Just think about how wonderful it will be to have peace, joy, and right standing with God, to be blessed and be able to be a blessing to others. Think of how great it will be to have healthy relationships, to be able to forgive quickly, to be confident, to see your prayers answered, and to experience dozens of other things that will bring joy to your heart. Don't delay; start today.

PART 3

The Beatitudes: Keys to Blessing

CHAPTER 17

The First and Second Beatitudes

Becoming a child is living the beatitudes and so finding the narrow gate into the Kingdom.

Henri J. M. Nouwen[33]

I would be remiss in writing about being blessed if I didn't write about the Beatitudes, which are found in Matthew 5:1–12 and are part of Jesus' Sermon on the Mount (Matthew 5–7). The English word *beatitude* means "complete happiness that comes from being blessed (= made holy) by God."[34] The Beatitudes each extol a certain attitude, or way of living. There are eight of them, and a blessing is attached to each one. To live as the Beatitudes teach us to live requires obedience to God and the help of the Holy Spirit.

Before we think about each Beatitude individually, let's first look at the entire Scripture passage:

> Now when Jesus saw the crowds, he went up on a mountainside and sat down. His disciples came to him, and he began to teach them. He said:
>
> "Blessed are the poor in spirit, for theirs is the kingdom of heaven.
>
> Blessed are those who mourn, for they will be comforted.
>
> Blessed are the meek, for they will inherit the earth.
>
> Blessed are those who hunger and thirst for righteousness, for they will be filled.
>
> Blessed are the merciful, for they will be shown mercy.
>
> Blessed are the pure in heart, for they will see God.
>
> Blessed are the peacemakers, for they will be called children of God.
>
> Blessed are those who are persecuted because of righteousness, for theirs is the kingdom of heaven.
>
> Blessed are you when people insult you, persecute you and falsely say all kinds of evil against you because of me. Rejoice and be glad, because great is your reward in

heaven, for in the same way they persecuted the prophets who were before you."

Matthew 5:1–12

Beatitudes are blessings pronounced on virtues God wants us to exhibit. According to Noah Webster's 1828 dictionary,[35] "The radical sense [of *virtue*] is strength, from straining, stretching, extending." The second and third definitions say, "bravery, valor... moral goodness; the practice of moral duties and the abstaining from vice." The third definition goes on to say, "In this sense, *virtue* may be, and in many instances must be, distinguished from religion."

Religion is often seen only in outward acts, whereas virtue is a matter of the heart. Webster's 1828 dictionary also notes, "VIRTUE is nothing but voluntary obedience to the truth" and further defines *virtue* as "a particular moral excellence; as the *virtue* of temperance, of chastity, of charity"; "acting power"; and "excellence; or that which constitutes value and merit."

If I were to try to summarize in my own words what I have learned about the Beatitudes, I would say that the Beatitudes are qualities of moral excellence obtained through obedience to God, based on a person's love for Him and to which special blessings are attached.

The character qualities mentioned in the Beatitudes are not easy to obtain, and they go against our natural human nature (who we are without God). However, all things are possible with God, and the Holy Spirit helps us obey God's Word, so we can live as Jesus instructs in Matthew 5:1–12. God changes us into the image of Christ, who had all these moral qualities.

Let's spend the remainder of this chapter looking at the first two Beatitudes. I've presented them earlier in this chapter in the New International Version of the Bible, but I'd like us to look at them individually in the Amplified Bible, Classic Edition, where each verse is more descriptive. I use this version on purpose because it offers so much insight into each verse, and I want you to fully realize what it means to be blessed. Among other things, it means we can have happiness (joy) regardless of our outward condition. We may also experience God's favor that is given us due to His grace. To be blessed is wonderful and amazing. We are blessed, and we should thank God each day for all the ways He blesses us.

1. Blessed Are the Poor in Spirit

> Blessed (happy, to be envied, and spiritually prosperous— with life-joy and satisfaction in God's favor and salvation, regardless of their outward conditions) are the poor in spirit (the humble, who rate themselves insignificant), for theirs is the kingdom of heaven!
>
> Matthew 5:3 AMPC

The poor in spirit are humble. They do not think more highly of themselves than they ought to. Rick Warren says, "Humility is not thinking less of yourself; it is thinking of yourself less."[36]

Although love is the highest virtue, many wise people of God assert that humility is considered the most difficult one to obtain and maintain, and I agree. Nevertheless, Scripture encourages us to live in humility before God and in our relationships with other people, and it promises blessings to those who do so. Ephesians 4:2 says: "Be completely humble and gentle; be patient, bearing with one another in love." Colossians 3:12 says: "Therefore, as God's chosen people, holy and dearly loved, clothe yourselves with compassion, kindness, humility, gentleness and patience." And 1 Peter 5:5 says, "God resists the proud, but gives grace to the humble" (NKJV).

Pride: The Opposite of Humility

I believe pride, which is the opposite of humility, is the root of all evil
and the beginning of sin.

> Pride is the root of all evil
> and the beginning of sin.

Satan was filled with pride and,
as a result, he was expelled from heaven (Ezekiel 28:17; Isaiah
14:12–15). He tries to lure us into pride and keep us from humility
because he knows the blessing that is attached to those who are
humble or, as Matthew 5:3 says, "poor in spirit." Pride causes us
to compare ourselves with other people, but those who are poor
in spirit avoid this because they see no need for comparison. The
humble do not compare themselves with anyone else because they
are content to be who God made them to be and to exercise the
gifts He has given them. They are not concerned with what people
think of them. Their joy is found in pleasing God alone.

The humble treat everyone with respect and are not concerned
merely for their own interests, but also for the interests of others.
If we humble ourselves, God will
lift us up (1 Peter 5:6). God wants
us to live in peace (2 Corinthians
13:11), and in order to maintain

> Peace is not possible without
> humility.

peace we must be willing and able to adapt and adjust ourselves to
others, but the proud cannot do that. Peace is not possible without humility.

God uses humble people who are pliable and moldable in His
hands. Pride comes before destruction (Proverbs 16:18). There
are many people mentioned in the Bible who were proud and
ultimately met their downfall or destruction, such as Uzziah (2
Chronicles 26:16–23) and Haman (Esther 6–7). King Nebuchadnezzar had to be demoted due to pride (Daniel 4:30–31); he lost
his mind and sunk so low that he lived in the fields and ate grass

with oxen for seven years until he returned to his right mind and humbled himself again (Daniel 4:28–37). And look at what happened to Herod Agrippa, who was eaten by worms because he did not give God glory when he should have:

> On the appointed day Herod, wearing his royal robes, sat on his throne and delivered a public address to the people. They shouted, "This is the voice of a god, not of a man." Immediately, because Herod did not give praise to God, an angel of the Lord struck him down, and he was eaten by worms and died.
>
> Acts 12:21–23

Pride deceived even Jesus' disciples, and they displayed it when they argued among themselves about which of them was the greatest (Luke 9:46).

> The antidote for pride is humility.

The antidote for pride is humility, and humility is a characteristic of the poor in spirit. It must be sought after with ardent zeal. It does not come easily, and it slips away without continual vigilance.

Be humble in your dealings with other people

Both humility and pride can be easily seen in the way people treat others. Those who have power over others often mistreat them, and God will avenge them. Treat all people well and respectfully, as Jesus did, especially the lowly, the poor, and the disadvantaged. God takes seriously—even personally—the way we treat people. Jesus says:

> "For I was hungry and you gave me nothing to eat, I was thirsty and you gave me nothing to drink, I was a stranger

and you did not invite me in, I needed clothes and you did not clothe me, I was sick and in prison and you did not look after me."

They also will answer, "Lord, when did we see you hungry or thirsty or a stranger or needing clothes or sick or in prison, and did not help you?"

He will reply, "Truly I tell you, whatever you did not do for one of the least of these, you did not do for me."

Matthew 25:42–45

Jesus says we should take His yoke upon us and learn from Him because He is "gentle (meek) and humble (lowly) in heart" (Matthew 11:29 AMPC). Jesus was good to people, especially those who were hurting, being mistreated, or poor. He always had time to stop, listen to, and help people.

2. Blessed Are Those Who Mourn

Blessed and enviably happy [with a happiness produced by the experience of God's favor and especially conditioned by the revelation of His matchless grace] are those who mourn, for they shall be comforted!

Matthew 5:4 AMPC

I believe "Blessed are those who mourn" means that God blesses those who have a tender heart. If we believe that God's grace and sovereignty are greater than any loss or disappointment, we can experience joy in the midst of sorrow.

> You can experience joy in the midst of sorrow.

The Beatitudes are prime examples of how we can be blessed amid our messes. Matthew 5:4 teaches us that the comfort of God is so wonderful that anything that causes us to mourn opens the door for the amazing blessing of comfort.

The Blessing of God's Comfort

I have known people who have endured tremendous tragedy yet remained peaceful, loving, and kind. Others have asked them, "How can you possibly go through what you have gone through and have such a great attitude?" One woman I know lost four of her children to a drowning accident, yet she was not angry or bitter, and she never lost her faith in God. She actually leaned into God even harder. God's grace and comfort were poured out on her, and it was evident that the comfort she felt was supernatural.

> Some people carry the pain of their loss and refuse to be comforted.

Mourning is a natural result of any kind of loss, but it should not become a permanent condition. Some people carry the pain of their loss and refuse to be comforted. Jacob refused to be comforted concerning the loss of Joseph. He said that he would go to his grave mourning Joseph, and he wept for him (Genesis 37:35). If you are mourning a loss right now, I encourage you to ask for and receive God's comfort.

According to 2 Corinthians 1:3–4, He is the God of all comfort:

> Praise be to the God and Father of our Lord Jesus Christ, the Father of compassion and the God of all comfort, who comforts us in all our troubles, so that we can comfort those in any trouble with the comfort we ourselves receive from God.

These verses say that when we experience God's comfort, we can comfort others with the comfort we have received. We are blessed indeed when we can pour out to others the comfort God has given us.

When Bad Things Happen to Good People

We often ask, "Why do bad things happen to good people?" But a better question would be "What happens to good people when bad things happen to them?" Here are some of the answers:

- They grow spiritually.
- They bounce back stronger than they were before.
- They get better, not bitter.
- They don't complain about what they have lost; they thank God for everything they still have.
- They continue obeying God.
- They continue being a blessing to others, even though they are hurting.
- They experience God's comfort.

It is hard to feel blessed when we have lost something. However, the things we cling to often separate us from a deeper relationship with God. In life, we discover that God can use what seems to be the worst tragedy to bring us closer to Him. For example, we might lose a relationship that is very important to us, but perhaps it is not one that is good for us. God, in His infinite wisdom, may separate us from that person because they would hold us back from what God wants us to do in life. We will eventually see that what we thought was tragic was actually a blessing.

Joseph was horribly mistreated by his brothers, yet he ended up saying, "As for you, you thought evil against me, but God meant it for good, to bring about that many people should be kept alive, as they are this day" (Genesis 50:20 AMPC).

The Folly of Self-Pity

Self-pity does not comfort us; it makes us increasingly miserable. If we want God's comfort, we
need to sacrifice feeling sorry for
ourselves.

> Self-pity makes you
> increasingly miserable.

Although we inflict pain on our-
selves when we waste our time feeling like victims or feeling sorry
for ourselves, we often choose to do so. I have finally learned that
I would rather have God's comfort than my own self-pity.

Self-pity is rooted in fear; when we suffer tragedy, loss, or disappointment, we tend to feel sorry for ourselves and are afraid we
will never get over it. We fear we will never get back what we have
lost and that we will forever feel the pain we currently feel. If we
refuse to be comforted, we may always feel the pain, but we do not
have to live this way. We can be pitiful or powerful, but we cannot
be both. It is our choice.

Here are several signs to help you recognize self-pity:

- Self-pity wants to blame someone for its troubles. Whether
  it's a human being or God, self-pity demands that someone
  be blamed.
- Self-pity is pessimistic. It assumes bad news will be followed
  by more bad news, and feeds on this negativity.
- People who feel self-pity can become so negative that they
  may resent anyone who tries to comfort or encourage them.
  If someone says, "God will comfort you and give you grace,"
  self-pity often becomes defensive. Someone engrossed in self-
  pity may tell a person trying to help, "You just don't understand how difficult things are for me."
- Self-pity wants sympathy, but sympathy is not true comfort.
- Self-pity talks and thinks incessantly about a problem.

- People who are filled with self-pity view themselves as worse off than anyone else. If you try to share a difficulty you are having, theirs is always much worse than yours.
- People who feel self-pity refuse advice that will help them get out of their situation.
- Self-pity is selfish because it turns us in on ourselves and we think about nothing except how we feel.
- Self-pity doesn't think much of situations other people endure but focuses intensely on what we're going through.

As I write this, I have a mess of my own. My back was injured, and I have great difficulty getting in and out of chairs. When I want to get up, I have to call Dave to help me get out of a chair. I am putting ice on my back and walking around the house for five minutes every thirty minutes as instructed by my chiropractor. Right now, even though I have prayed and asked others to pray for me, I seem to be getting worse instead of better. In five days, I need to be at my granddaughter's wedding in Georgia, and two days after that I am scheduled to preach at a church in Georgia.

What-if scenarios keep playing in my mind, and I must chase them off while still waiting on God to show me what course of action to take. I would prefer to have a miraculous healing, but God may not give me the easy way. I may have to go a route I would rather not take. I might need a shot in my back, an MRI, or physical therapy, none of which I feel I have time for right now. I don't know all the answers yet, but I do know that feeling sorry for myself or trying hard to understand why this happened to me right now won't do any good. I need to wait patiently on God while trusting Him, and I need to continue helping others as much as I can. Above all else, I need to hope in God and believe He will enable me to keep all my commitments.

Find Comfort in Hope

One way God comforts us is by giving us hope. Hope is an expectation that God will do something good in our life. People who are filled with hope wait on God expectantly with a positive attitude. They believe God will work out their problem for their good (Romans 8:28). They also believe that they can do whatever they need to do through Christ, who is their strength (Philippians 4:13).

> God comforts you by giving you hope.

People who have a positive attitude believe that God will never allow more to come on them than they can bear and that He will always provide a way out of situations that cause them to feel trapped (1 Corinthians 10:13). Any time I say to Dave, "I can't take any more of this," he reminds me of this scripture.

God promises to be with us in trouble, and people with a positive attitude believe this. Consider what God says in Psalm 91:15: "He will call on me, and I will answer him; I will be with him in trouble, I will deliver him and honor him." Psalm 34:19 says, "The righteous person may have many troubles, but the Lord delivers him from them all."

God obviously wants to comfort us in our difficulties, because in addition to His comforting us, He has sent the Holy Spirit, "the Comforter," to live in us, according to John 16:7 (AMPC):

> However, I am telling you nothing but the truth when I say it is profitable (good, expedient, advantageous) for you that I go away. Because if I do not go away, the Comforter (Counselor, Helper, Advocate, Intercessor, Strengthener, Standby) will not come to you [into close fellowship with you]; but if I go away, I will send Him to you [to be in close fellowship with you].

If you have experienced a painful loss in your life, let me assure you that I know how difficult it is, and I have compassion for you. But I also want you to know that God's comfort is available to you. We can find great comfort as we take to heart Jesus' encouraging words: "Ask and you will receive, and your joy will be complete" (John 16:24).

God desires to help us in all our troubles, and the blessing of His comfort is one way He does this. God can give us the peace that passes understanding in the midst of our most difficult and painful situations (Philippians 4:7). He loves you, and you can trust Him to give you a double blessing for your former trouble (Isaiah 61:7).

> God can give you the peace that passes understanding in the midst of your most painful situations.

Receiving God's Comfort When You Have Sinned

Those of us who truly love God mourn and grieve when we sin, especially if the sin has significant consequences. But remember, those who mourn are blessed and will be comforted, according to Matthew 5:4. All sin is bad, but some sins bother us more than others do. If someone loses their temper and behaves badly, it is sin. But if they repent, their peace is restored quickly. If, however, they were to commit adultery or steal something, those actions would probably be more difficult to get over.

When we sin, we must remember that Jesus came to set us free from all sin and its guilt. Through Him, we can resist sin. But if we fail to resist, we can still be completely forgiven when we do sin. Sin often brings unpleasant results in our lives, and I am not saying that forgiveness delivers us from all its consequences, but God will forgive us no matter what we have done if we are truly repentant. We should remember that God never stops loving us.

Think about these words of the psalmist David:

Blessed is the one whose transgressions are forgiven, whose sins are covered. Blessed is the one whose sin the Lord does not count against them and in whose spirit is no deceit.

Psalm 32:1–2

If you have made a big mistake, you are not alone. King David, who wrote Psalm 32:1–2, committed adultery with Bathsheba and then had her husband killed (2 Samuel 11:1–17). David was a man who was close to God, but the weakness of his flesh overpowered him, and he did a terrible thing. Yet, God forgave him. His house was never without war after that (2 Samuel 12:10), but he was forgiven.

In closing this chapter, I want to encourage you to receive God's forgiveness and to forgive yourself. Refusing to receive the forgiveness and comfort God offers does no good at all and will not fix a bad situation. Had God not wanted you to be comforted, He would not be called "the God of all comfort." If you are mourning over something, receive God's comfort and move on with your life, because He has many good things in store for you.

CHAPTER 18

The Third and Fourth Beatitudes

The unthankful heart...discovers no mercies; but let the thankful heart sweep through the day and, as the magnet finds the iron, so it will find, in every hour, some heavenly blessings!

Henry Ward Beecher[37]

L et's continue our study of the Beatitudes as we move further away from the messes in our lives and closer to greater blessings. In this chapter, we'll look at two more types of people Jesus calls blessed.

3. Blessed Are the Meek

Blessed (happy, blithesome, joyous, spiritually prosperous—with life-joy and satisfaction in God's favor and salvation, regardless of their outward conditions) are the meek (the mild, patient, long-suffering), for they shall inherit the earth!

Matthew 5:5 AMPC

To be meek is to be gentle, humble, and lowly. People who are meek do not assert themselves over others to further their own agendas. To "inherit the earth" means to enjoy the blessings of our temporal life on earth and of eternal life in heaven. Meekness is often misunderstood as weakness, but it is actually strength under control.

> Meekness is not weakness but strength under control.

Jesus was meek, but He had all power. We see a good example of His meekness when Judas and the soldiers approached Him to arrest Him in the Garden of Gethsemane. Peter took up his sword and cut off the ear of one of the high priest's servants (John 18:10). Jesus simply said to Peter, "Put your sword back in its place.... Do you think I cannot call on my Father, and he will at once put at my disposal more than twelve legions of angels?" (Matthew

26:52–53). Twelve legions of angels would be about 72,000 angels. That's a *lot*, but Jesus said He could ask God for even more than that, and they would rush to His aid.

Why did Jesus not ask for the angels? Why did He stand by meekly and allow Himself to be mistreated? Because He came to earth to do the Father's will, not His own. He said, "But how then would the Scriptures be fulfilled that say it must happen this way?" (Matthew 26:54). To have power and be able to restrain it requires meekness. Meekness is an attitude that says, "I will wait on God and not take matters into my own hands."

> *Meekness says, "I will wait on God and not take matters into my own hands."*

We see another picture of Jesus' meekness in 1 Peter 2:21, where Peter writes about the example Jesus set for us through His suffering. In this context, he says, "When they hurled their insults at him, he did not retaliate; when he suffered, he made no threats. Instead, he entrusted himself to him who judges justly" (1 Peter 2:23).

Jesus could have easily put a stop to the wrong that was being done to Him, but He didn't. He waited on and trusted in His Father. I find it difficult not to retaliate when someone insults me or mistreats me, don't you? Our first thought may be, *Surely, we are not called to just let people walk all over us.* God certainly doesn't want us to be mistreated, but when we are, He does want us to wait on Him to vindicate us instead of taking revenge ourselves. Think about this Scripture passage:

> *When you are mistreated, wait on God to vindicate you.*

> For it is commendable if someone bears up under the pain
> of unjust suffering because they are conscious of God. But
> how is it to your credit if you receive a beating for doing

wrong and endure it? But if you suffer for doing good and you endure it, this is commendable before God. To this you were called, because Christ suffered for you, leaving you an example, that you should follow in his steps.

1 Peter 2:19–21

I must admit that I find these scriptures difficult to get excited about, but after many years of experience with God and studying His Word, I do understand that people who behave as this passage describes are not weak and incapable. They are people of great strength and power, yet they restrain themselves from exerting it and instead wait on God to bring justice in their life, as these scriptures promise:

Do not take revenge, my dear friends, but leave room for God's wrath, for it is written: "It is mine to avenge; I will repay," says the Lord.

Romans 12:19

For we know Him Who said, Vengeance is Mine [retribution and the meting out of full justice rest with Me]; I will repay [I will exact the compensation], says the Lord. And again, The Lord will judge and determine and solve and settle the cause and the cases of His people.

Hebrews 10:30 AMPC

Quite often when I have been mistreated and know I need to wait on God to vindicate me, I turn to these scriptures and let them strengthen me, enabling me to do His will instead of mine.

The power of restraint may be the greatest power of all. If we will

> Restraint may be the greatest power of all.

wait on God when we are mistreated, the vindication He gives will be much sweeter than any we could ever obtain for ourselves.

There are times to speak up and not allow people to take advantage of us, but we should do this only when it is for their good, not ours. Parents must train children. Employers must set standards for their employees to follow. Jesus, in righteous anger, overturned the tables of the money changers because they were defiling the temple of God (Matthew 21:12–13). In this case, His indignation was stirred up because of the disrespect being shown to His Father's house, not because He was trying to defend Himself.

Often when Jesus was accused of doing wrong, He did not offer even one word in His own defense (Matthew 27:12). The Bible says: "As a sheep before its shearers is silent, so he did not open his mouth" (Isaiah 53:7). Yes, Jesus was meek, and we are to follow His example. Although it is difficult to understand, it is true that the meeker people are, the more powerful they are.

Are You a Laborer or an Inheritor?

The meek inherit the earth; they are inheritors. In contrast, those who take matters into their own hands and do not wait on God are laborers. They constantly strive to get what they want, and their efforts only end in frustration. I know because I wasted many years laboring instead of inheriting. I frustrated myself trying to do what only God could do. I tried to change myself and other people. I tried to make people treat me the way I thought they should. I tried to make my ministry grow. As I often say, "I tried until I almost died," but it did no good.

> Be content with what you have while you wait on God to give you more.

God wants us to be content with what we have while we wait on Him to give us more—in His timing and in His way. People who are meek are blessed because they are content. The blessedness of contentment is too wonderful to be explained; you simply have to experience it. Paul "learned to be content" (Philippians 4:11–12), so contentment must be something we *learn*, not a quality we naturally possess. Sadly, I think the only way we learn to be content is by trying to make things happen ourselves and failing, being frustrated, and growing weary. Hopefully, we finally see the foolishness of our ways and give them up in favor of doing things God's way.

We give our children advice, yet they often must find out for themselves that what we were telling them was right. God is the same way with us. He has given us His Word, and in it we find instruction for daily living, but we usually have to find out for ourselves the hard way that God's ways are truly blessed ways.

God gives us blessings we cannot earn or buy with our works (fleshly efforts in our own strength). He gives peace, joy, deep satisfaction, and a sense of being in right standing with Him. He gives us the understanding that apart from Him we can do nothing (John 15:5), and we learn to ask for what we want and need and wait on Him to give it to us if it is His will.

A Key to Getting from Where You Are to Where You Want to Be

Receiving correction is the pathway to growth and advancement. When we want to move forward but are stuck where we are, it's usually because we are doing something we should not be doing, or we are *not* doing something we should be doing. We cannot correct a problem if we don't know it exists, so

> *Receiving correction is the pathway to growth and advancement.*

God helps us by showing us our weaknesses. He does this because He loves us. Hebrews 12:5–6 says:

And have you completely forgotten this word of encouragement that addresses you as a father addresses his son? It says, "My son, do not make light of the Lord's discipline, and do not lose heart when he rebukes you, because the Lord disciplines the one he loves, and he chastens everyone he accepts as his son."

God corrects us Himself if we will accept His correction. But if we won't, He will try to correct us through someone else. Our son once told Dave and me that we had never corrected him about anything that the Lord had not been dealing with him about before we mentioned it.

We should not view correction as negative, but as positive. It's "right direction." When we need correction, it's because things in our lives are not working out well and we need to go in a different direction. When we ask God to help us and He does so by showing us the error of our ways, we may resist it because we don't want to think we are doing anything wrong. We usually don't want to have to change; we just want God to magically make our problems go away.

God does try to get our attention and help us with our problems, but if that does not work, He will touch our circumstances. When our children were young, I always tried first to talk them into behaving, but if they continued to misbehave, I had to discipline them by doing something that affected their circumstances. They lost a privilege or were punished in some other way, but I did it for their good because I loved them. Often, their correction hurt me more than it hurt them. As parents, we love our children and don't want to see them suffer, but we may temporarily apply something that is not pleasant for them in order to prevent them from continuing to do something that will cause them to suffer permanently.

In the Old Testament story of the prophet Jonah, God told Jonah what to do: "Go to the great city of Nineveh and preach against it, because its wickedness has come up before me" (Jonah 1:2). But Jonah went to Tarshish, a city in the opposite direction from where God told him to go (Jonah 1:3). I believe he simply did not want to go and preach to the people of Nineveh because he felt they were undeserving. As he sailed toward Tarshish, the ship ran into a terrible storm. When Jonah admitted to the people aboard the ship with him that he was the reason for the storm (Jonah 1:8–10), they threw him overboard (Jonah 1:15). In the sea, he was swallowed by a large fish that God had provided to rescue him (Jonah 1:17).

From the belly of the fish, Jonah cried out to God. He prayed, repented for his disobedience, and said he would keep his vow to obey Him (Jonah 2:1–9). God caused the fish to spit him out on dry ground (Jonah 2:10), but I am sure the experience was totally awful. It's a shame that God had to go to such lengths to get Jonah to obey Him, but He did. Jonah finally did as the Lord commanded (Jonah 3:3), even though it seemed wrong to him (Jonah 4:1).

Sometimes, we can be like Jonah when God asks us to do something we don't think is fair, but obedience is always the best way to go. God will ultimately get His way, but we can make it easy or difficult on ourselves. As you grow in meekness, you will see God take situations you may view as negative and turn them into blessings. The meek will inherit the earth.

4. Blessed Are Those Who Hunger and Thirst for Righteousness

Blessed and fortunate and happy and spiritually prosperous (in that state in which the born-again child of God enjoys His favor and salvation) are those who hunger and thirst for righteousness (uprightness and right standing with God), for they shall be completely satisfied!

Matthew 5:6 AMPC

In the Living Bible, this verse reads, "Happy are those who long to be just and good, for they shall be completely satisfied."

We have all experienced being hungry or thirsty at times. When this happens, we crave either food or drink. We feel we need them for our very survival. This beatitude describes not simply an interest in righteousness (which means being rightly related to God). We are to *hunger* and *thirst* for it—have a recognition of our deep spiritual need for righteousness. Psalm 42:1–2 provides a picture of this: "As the deer pants for streams of water, so my soul pants for you, my God. My soul thirsts for God, for the living God. When can I go and meet with God?"

As we read Psalm 42:1–2, we can almost feel the psalmists' desperation for God. We also hunger and thirst for Him. We can keep this verse in mind as we think about hungering and thirsting for righteousness.

Understanding Righteousness

There are two kinds of righteousness, and we need to make sure we seek the godly one—the only one that works. Otherwise, we will not be satisfied. Paul prayed that he would be found in Christ, "not having a righteousness of my own that comes from the law, but that which is through faith in Christ—the righteousness that comes from God on the basis of faith" (Philippians 3:9). From this scripture, we see that there are two types of righteousness:

- Righteousness that comes from obeying the law. This would require perfect obedience to the law, which no person can do.

- Righteousness that is imputed (given) to us through faith in Christ.

Which of these two sounds easier? Of course, the second is easier, but we tend to try to obtain righteousness first by being good and doing good. However, this never works. It only leaves us frustrated. I remember frequently telling God in certain situations that I was "trying" so hard and didn't know what else I could do. I desperately wanted to be and do all that God wanted of me. I hungered and thirsted for righteousness, but like many people, I tried to get it in ways that didn't work.

In Old Testament times, God gave the law, which set forth His perfect standards of righteousness. If anyone could keep the law in its entirety, that person would be right with God, but it is impossible for anyone to follow it completely. In fact, God gave the law to show us that we *could not* keep it, thereby leading us to trust in Jesus' atoning sacrifice to make us righteous in Him (Romans 3:20–25; Galatians 3:19–27).

Under the Old Testament law, animal sacrifices were required regularly. The blood of these sacrifices "covered" the sin of the people, but they were never free from the guilt of their sin. The sacrificial system was like sweeping dirt under the rug. Sin was covered, but people always knew it was still there.

The fact that no one can keep the law completely reveals humanity's need for a Savior. Under the New Covenant, Jesus sacrificed Himself as payment for our sins. His blood not only covers sin, but it cleanses our sin and removes the guilt sin causes. Christ's sacrifice must be received by faith and faith alone. We cannot earn the gift of righteousness and forgiveness through good works or by any other means. Second Corinthians 5:21 (AMPC) helps us understand this:

For our sake He made Christ [virtually] to be sin Who knew no sin, so that in and through Him we might become [endued with, viewed as being in, and examples of] the righteousness of God [what we ought to be, approved and acceptable and in right relationship with Him, by His goodness].

When Have I Done Enough?

Our ministry once took a survey to see what question people would ask God if they could ask only one. The number one question people wanted to ask God—above all others—was "How can I know when I have done enough?" This is interesting. As believers in Jesus, we do want to please Him. This desire is commendable, and God delights in it. To hunger and thirst for righteousness refers to the intensity with which one desires to live righteously. In other words, it is not merely a faint hope but an intense desire to please God, one that is strong enough to affect our behavior. If we want strongly enough to live in a godly way, we will try to make sacrifices or do whatever it takes to do so. This may seem noble, but it isn't what God desires. He doesn't want our effort;

> God wants your faith, not your effort.

He wants our faith. He wants us to trust Him to do in and for us what we cannot do ourselves, even though we try.

The moment a person is born again, they become new in Christ (2 Corinthians 5:17). Jesus takes their sin and gives them His righteousness. Second Corinthians 5:21 says, "God made him who had no sin to be sin for us, so that in him we might become the righteousness of God." In other words, we are made right with God not through our effort but through Jesus' sacrifice.

But when Christ came into the world, He gave Himself, and by His "sacrifice he has made perfect forever those who are being made holy" (Hebrews 10:14). Right standing with God is His gift to us when we are born again, and He sends His Holy Spirit to work it out in our lives as we grow in Him.

God never expects us to produce something unless He first gives it to us. Because He makes us righteous, we can behave as He would have us to behave. Because He makes us holy, we can grow in holiness. Because He forgives us, we can forgive others. And because He is merciful to us, we can show mercy to others.

We must realize who we are in Christ, understand what He has given us, and receive it by faith before we can do what He wants us to do. In God's economy, we believe first, and then we see. This is what faith is. "Faith is confidence in what we hope for and assurance about what we do not see" (Hebrews 11:1).

Sources differ regarding how many promises God's Word includes, but as best I can tell, there are between five and seven thousand promises in the Bible. In order to receive each one of them as a reality in our life, we must first believe by faith (without seeing) that they truly are ours.

So the answer to the question "When have I done enough?" is this: You have done enough when you sincerely believe.

CHAPTER 19

The Fifth and Sixth Beatitudes

I have always found that mercy bears richer fruits than strict justice.

Abraham Lincoln[38]

I hope you're beginning to see what great blessings are available to us in Christ. The Beatitudes promise many good and desirable things to us as we live according to Jesus' teachings. In this chapter, let's look at two more qualities we will cultivate in our lives if we want to be blessed—mercy and purity of heart.

5. Blessed Are the Merciful

Blessed (happy, to be envied, and spiritually prosperous—with life-joy and satisfaction in God's favor and salvation, regardless of their outward conditions) are the merciful, for they shall obtain mercy!

Matthew 5:7 AMPC

We all need a lot of mercy because we all make a lot of mistakes. The best way to be given mercy is to generously give it away. First, we receive mercy from God, and then He expects us to let it flow through us to others. Mercy cannot be deserved or earned. It is a gift to the undeserving. Lamentations 3:22–23 tells us that God's mercies "are new every morning" (NKJV). I am so thankful for this, and I'm sure you are too.

Matthew 9:10–13 tells the story of a dinner that took place at Matthew's house. Jesus and His disciples were eating there, along with "many tax collectors and sinners" (v. 10). Let's look at what happened:

When the Pharisees saw this, they asked his disciples, "Why does your teacher eat with tax collectors and sinners?" On hearing this, Jesus said, "It is not the healthy who need a doctor, but the sick. But go and learn what this

means: 'I desire mercy, not sacrifice.' For I have not come
to call the righteous, but sinners."

Matthew 9:11–13

Jesus came to give us mercy, not to require sacrifice, and He wants
us to give mercy to others and not require sacrifice of them. Mercy is
a beautiful thing. It instantly takes pressure off people who may mistakenly think God requires certain
behaviors from them, but they don't
know how to demonstrate what they
think He wants.

> Jesus wants you to give
> mercy to others, not require
> sacrifice of them.

I looked up "What is the biblical
meaning of mercy?" on the internet, and the answer that came up
was one word: *forgiveness*. The information I found went on to say,
"Mercy appears in the Bible as it relates to forgiveness or with-
holding punishment."

The biblical concept of mercy goes beyond forgiveness and with-
holding punishment. For example, God shows His mercy toward
those who are suffering, but through healing and comfort, the suffering may be alleviated. In the original languages of the Bible,
there are at least four words for the English word *mercy*.[39] Sum-
marized in simple terms, the Hebrew word *chesed* (Strong's #2617)
means "unfailing love, kindness, tenderness," and *racham* (Strong's
#7355), used in the context of "to have mercy," means "to show
compassion, pity, love." In Greek, *eleos* (Strong's #1656) means "an
expression of pity," and *eleeo* (Strong's #1653), used in the context
of "to have mercy," means "active desire to remove distress."

I have read that mercy is kindness in excess of what may be
expected or demanded by fairness. Mercy doesn't just do what is
fair. Mercy is extravagant; it goes beyond reason.

Mercy is closely related to compassion, and I am always struck
by the fact that Jesus was "moved with compassion" (Matthew

9:36 NKJV; 14:14 NKJV; Mark 1:41 NKJV). He didn't merely feel sorry for hurting people; He always did something to help them. It is wonderful to know that God will help us when we don't deserve it and that He enables us to help others who don't deserve it.

When people treat us unjustly or make mistakes, God wants us to show them mercy, not try to make them pay for their misdeeds. Retaliation is part of our old nature, but our new nature is that of Christ Himself. He says, "Freely you have received; freely give" (Matthew 10:8).

> *Show mercy to those who treat you unjustly or make mistakes.*

We Reap What We Sow

The Bible warns us:

> Do not be deceived, God is not mocked; for whatever a man sows, that he will also reap. For he who sows to his flesh will of the flesh reap corruption, but he who sows to the Spirit will of the Spirit reap everlasting life. And let us not grow weary while doing good, for in due season we shall reap if we do not lose heart.
>
> Galatians 6:7–9 NKJV

The fact that people reap what they sow is a law of nature and a law of God. We can easily understand this principle by thinking of gardening or farming. If a farmer sows tomato seeds, he won't get pumpkins. If he sows seeds that are rotten, he won't reap healthy fruit. This is a natural law that God has set into motion since the beginning of time. As long as the earth remains, there will be seedtime and harvest (Genesis 8:22).

Before reminding us that we reap what we sow, Galatians 6:7 tells us not to be deceived and think it won't happen. Sowing and reaping can't be avoided. If we want or need more of something, all we need to do is sow some of it. Even a little seed can produce a giant harvest.

Jesus tells a short parable in Matthew 13:31–32:

> The kingdom of heaven is like a mustard seed, which a man took and planted in his field. Though it is the smallest of all seeds, yet when it grows, it is the largest of garden plants and becomes a tree, so that the birds come and perch in its branches.

This teaches us that those who listen to God's Word and follow it will reap the kingdom of heaven. The blessing far outweighs the sacrifice of the seed.

We should not sow what we do not want to reap. Jesus says, "Do not judge, and you will not be judged. Do not condemn, and you will not be condemned" (Luke 6:37). He goes on in this passage to remind us again, this time in a positive sense, that we reap what we sow: "Forgive, and you will be forgiven. Give, and it will be given to you. A good measure, pressed down, shaken together and running over, will be poured into your lap. For with the measure you use, it will be measured to you" (Luke 6:37–38).

> Do not sow what you do not want to reap.

The Blessing of Caring for Others

In the Message Bible, Matthew 5:7 reads this way: "You're blessed when you care. At the moment of being 'care-full,' you find yourselves cared for."

I have discovered that one of the best things we can do in life is to

> Help others, not just those deserving of it but those who are not.

help and care for other people—not just those deserving of help, but perhaps especially those who are not.

Selfishness leads to unhappiness, and selfish people do not care about anyone except themselves. If they do care for others, they don't care as much for them as they do for themselves.

Mercy does not look only at what a person has done but takes time to see why they did it. I behaved badly in the earlier years of my life, due to sexual, emotional, and mental abuse during my childhood. People only saw my behavior, but God saw the *why* behind *what* I did. A hard-hearted person deals only with facts, but mercy sees a person's heart.

Mercy sees a person's heart.

A merciful person has come face-to-face with their own wretchedness in the sight of God. They know that, without His mercy, they would be consumed (Lamentations 3:22–23), so they find showing mercy to others easy. They are glad to give mercy because they know that probably before the day is finished, they will need mercy themselves.

I spent many years being totally selfish, and I was unhappy all the time. As God made me aware of how selfish I was and began teaching me the power of caring for others, my life changed drastically for the better. I personally discovered how happy caring for others made me, and I believe you'll find it makes you happy too. Some people have a gift of mercy, meaning that being merciful comes naturally to them. But some of us don't have that gift and have to develop the habit of showing mercy, remembering that God gives us mercy all the time.

James 2:13 says, "Mercy triumphs over judgment." I would rather be guilty of being too merciful than of being too judgmental. Paul teaches us in Colossians 3:12 to "put on" mercy (NKJV). Just as we choose and put on our clothes, we can choose and put on "[behavior marked by] tenderhearted pity and mercy, kind feeling," humble attitudes, "gentle ways, [and] patience," which, according to Colossians 3:12, "[is tireless and long-suffering, and has the power to endure whatever comes, with good temper]" (AMPC).

We confront many situations in which we need to make choices, and we should seek to make the

> I would rather be guilty of being too merciful than of being too judgmental.

ones Jesus would make. He always helped people who came to Him. He took time for them, no matter what else He was doing or where He was going. Let's make sure we don't act like the priest and the Levite in the story of the Good Samaritan, who passed by a man who had been beaten and robbed and lay in the road bleeding (Luke 10:30–32). He needed help, and though both of these men were religious, they passed by on the other side of the road and walked past him without helping him. I believe this passage of Scripture indicates that they crossed over to the other side of the road on purpose, and I think they did so because they didn't want to see the man. They could have even been rushing to the synagogue, and if so, it would make the tragedy even worse.

Are we guilty of being like the priest and the Levite sometimes? Do we find ways to close our eyes to the pain around us so that we don't feel guilty about not showing mercy or offering to help people? It's so easy to make the excuse that we are too busy. But if helping others is part of our purpose in being alive and we are too busy to do it, we may be missing out on much more than we realize. Helping others always deposits a blessing into our lives. It seems that most of us are always in a hurry, but I recently read somewhere that we cannot love if we are in a hurry. This is because when we are rushed, we often don't

> You cannot love if you are in a hurry.

even see the needs in front of us. Or, if we do see them, we are in too much of a hurry to stop and help. We all need to learn to slow down.

As you think about being merciful and looking for opportunities to show mercy to others, remember Proverbs 3:3–4: "Let not mercy and truth forsake you; bind them around your neck, write them on the tablet of your heart, and so find favor and high esteem in the sight of God and man" (NKJV). Remember also that a person who is merciful "does good for his own soul" (Proverbs 11:17 NKJV). Don't miss out on the blessing of giving and showing mercy.

6. Blessed Are the Pure in Heart

Blessed (happy, enviably fortunate, and spiritually prosperous—possessing the happiness produced by the experience of God's favor and especially conditioned by the revelation of His grace, regardless of their outward conditions) are the pure in heart, for they shall see God!

Matthew 5:8 AMPC

Those who are pure in heart are blessed to see God. This doesn't mean they see God with their natural eyes, because according to 1 John 4:12, "No one has ever seen God." It means they see God working in their lives and have a close relationship with Him that grants them the privilege of being easily led by His Spirit and hearing Him. This also means that the pure in heart will see God in heaven.

I also think those who are pure in heart possess a pure faith in God. They know He is with them, and they put their trust in Him. They walk in obedience to His commands by faith, believing that the blessings attached to obedience will be theirs.

Matthew Henry, in his commentary, says that Matthew 5:8 is "the most comprehensive of all the Beatitudes; here holiness and happiness are fully described and put together."[40] He goes on to say, "Here is the most comprehensive character of the blessed; they are *pure in heart*.... True Christianity lies in the heart, in the purity of the heart."[41]

You may wonder, *What does it mean to be "pure in heart"?* The New Testament was originally written in Greek, so it helps us to understand what *pure* and *heart* mean in the original language in which the Sermon on the Mount was recounted.

The Greek word used for *pure* in Matthew 5:8 is *katharos*. This word means "clean, pure." Physically, it includes: "purified by fire" and "like a vine cleansed by pruning and so fitted to bear fruit." Ethically, its meanings include "free from corrupt desire, from sin and guilt; blameless, innocent" and "unstained from the guilt of anything."[42]

The Greek word for *heart* in Matthew 5:8 is *kardia*. This word refers to "the physical organ of the body" and to "the seat of one's personal life (both physical and spiritual)." It is also "the seat of feelings, desires, joy, pain, and love. It is also the center for thought, understanding, and will."[43] One way I describe the heart is to say that it is the core of our being, the essence of who we are. Based on the definitions of *pure* and *heart*, I think we could say that to be pure in heart would be to be clean, blameless, and unstained by guilt in the core of our being.

One source I consulted about the meaning of being pure in heart says: "Being pure in heart involves having a singleness of heart toward God. A pure heart has no hypocrisy, no guile, no hidden motives. The pure heart is marked by transparency and an uncompromising desire to please God in all things. It is more than an *external* purity of behavior; it is an *internal* purity of soul."[44]

You and I cannot make our own hearts pure. We are made pure and righteous before God through Christ's work on our behalf. His sacrifice on the cross makes cleansing and purity possible for us. All we must do is receive it by faith.

When I think of being pure in heart, a scripture that comes to mind is Psalm 51. The background of this psalm is that David had committed adultery with Bathsheba and then had her husband killed. I am sure he felt guilty and unclean because of this, and he said to God:

> Have mercy on me, O God, according to your unfailing love; according to your great compassion blot out my transgressions. Wash away all my iniquity and cleanse me from my sin.... Hide your face from my sins and blot out all my iniquity. Create in me a pure heart, O God, and renew a steadfast spirit within me.
>
> Psalm 51:1–2, 9–10

Again, I will say: We cannot make ourselves pure in heart. But when we confess our sin and ask His forgiveness, God is faithful and will cleanse our hearts and then see us as pure before Him.

> *When you confess your sins, God forgives you and sees you as pure before Him.*

Pure-Hearted and Powerful

God is seeking people who are pure in heart (Matthew 5:8). A person who has a pure heart, who is wholeheartedly serving God, is truly powerful. In Psalm 51:6, David teaches us that having a pure heart means having truth in our "inner being" (AMPC), which is who we really are deep in our hearts. Having a pure heart starts with paying attention to our thoughts, because from our thoughts come our words, our emotions, our attitudes, and our motives.

It took me a long time to realize that God will not bless actions that are done out of wrong motives or an impure heart.

Purity of heart is not a natural trait; in most of us, it is something we must work on. First Thessalonians 4:3 teaches us to desire and work toward purity of heart because it is God's will. This is a challenge that every believer should be excited about accepting, but we do not have to face it alone. God has created us to be dependent upon Him, to take Him our challenges and allow Him to help us with them. Only He knows what is in our hearts, and He is an expert at removing the worthless things from us while retaining the valuable.

> *Purity of heart is not a natural trait but something you must work on.*

There is a price to pay to have a pure heart, but there is also a reward. We do not have to be afraid to make the commitment to allow God to do a deep purifying work in us. We may not always feel comfortable about the truth He brings us, but if we do our part—facing it, accepting it, and allowing it to change us—He will make sure we are blessed.

Motives

Our motives refer to *why* we do *what* we do. Jesus says that if we do good works so other people will see us, we lose our reward (Matthew 6:1). We should never do good works to get anything for ourselves. Our motive for the good things we do should be to obey God because we love Him and because we want to be a blessing to others. Any work we do that is not pure will be burned up on Judgment Day, and we will lose the reward that would have come as a result of the work had it been pure (1 Corinthians 3:12–15). I encourage you to ask God frequently to purify your heart, because the person who has a pure heart is among the happiest on the earth.

CHAPTER 20

The Seventh and Eighth Beatitudes

It isn't enough to talk about peace. One must believe in it. And it isn't enough to believe in it. One must work at it.

Eleanor Roosevelt[45]

I trust you are growing spiritually and moving toward greater blessings in your life as you study the lessons Jesus teaches in the Beatitudes. In this chapter, we'll look at the final two Beatitudes and learn about peace and how to stand strong and receive the blessings that come when we are persecuted for our faith.

7. Blessed Are Those Who Make and Maintain Peace

> Blessed (enjoying enviable happiness, spiritually prosperous—with life-joy and satisfaction in God's favor and salvation, regardless of their outward conditions) are the makers and maintainers of peace, for they shall be called the sons of God!
>
> Matthew 5:9 AMPC

We can pray for peace and wish for peace, but we won't have peace until we learn to make peace and maintain it. Being a peacemaker requires spiritual maturity. People who are spiritually mature could be defined as those who no longer act based on how they feel, what they think, or what they want, but they are obedient to God's Word in every possible way. Jesus says in Matthew 5:9 that people who make and maintain peace will be called "the sons of God" (AMPC). We are all children of God, but those who are sons and daughters are mature. They have grown spiritually to the degree that they behave like God, their Father.

Being a peacemaker requires spiritual maturity.

Those who are immature are referred to in the Bible as worldly or governed by the flesh (Romans 8:6–7; 1 Corinthians 3:3). Satan can easily steal the peace of anyone who walks in the flesh, following the impulses of human nature. It will be difficult, if not impossible, for this person to be a peacemaker because doing so requires humility, and humility is a fruit of the Spirit seen in the life of those who are spiritually mature (Galatians 5:22–23 AMPC).

> Humility is a fruit of the Spirit.

Just as a baby matures into a child and then an adult, Christians start out as babies and grow into children of God. Let's look at what Paul writes in 1 Corinthians 3:1–3:

> Brothers and sisters, I could not address you as people who live by the Spirit but as people who are still worldly—mere infants in Christ. I gave you milk, not solid food, for you were not yet ready for it. Indeed, you are still not ready. You are still worldly. For since there is jealousy and quarreling among you, are you not worldly? Are you not acting like mere humans?

Paul addresses his readers as "mere infants" because they cannot get along with one another. There is no peace because they are not mature enough to be peacemakers. Peacemakers are powerful. I often say, "Where there is no peace, there is no power. But when we know peace, we know power."

Anyone can be angry. All they need to do is follow their feelings, and as soon as they are offended or don't get their way, their anger flares up. Anger does not produce the righteousness that God desires (James 1:20). Spiritually mature believers want to live to please God. And no matter how hard it is, they will behave in a godly way and be the ones who take the first step to make peace. Are you willing to be the first one to say "I'm sorry"? Are you willing to give up your "right" to be right? Are you willing not to have the last word in a disagreement? Will you be the one to step up and say "Let's work this out and have peace between us"? These are important questions to ask on the path to spiritual maturity.

Before Jesus went to heaven after His time on earth, He said, "Peace I leave with you; my peace I give you" (John 14:27). Then He went on, in the same verse, to say, "Do not let your hearts be troubled and do not be afraid." This sentence in the Amplified Bible, Classic Edition says: "Stop allowing yourselves to be agitated and disturbed."

The apostle Paul urges us in 2 Timothy 2:23: "Don't have anything to do with foolish and stupid arguments, because you know they produce quarrels." This is great advice. In the Amplified Bible, Classic Edition, this verse reads: "But refuse (shut your mind against, have nothing to do with) trifling (ill-informed, unedifying, stupid) controversies over ignorant questionings, for you know that they foster strife and breed quarrels." It cannot be said any plainer than this.

Many of the things we argue about are petty. When I think back over the fifty-five years Dave and I have been married, as of the writing of this book, I sadly remember arguing about a lot of petty things. In the early years of our marriage, we did not know the value and power of peace as we know it now.

Know Peace, Know Power

In the Book of Acts, we see the early church operating in a power we seldom experience today, but they also lived and worked in unity (Acts 4:32). They shared all things with one another and lived in peace. They had problems, as all people do, but they confronted and solved them.

One time an argument arose regarding the feeding of the widows. The Hellenistic Jews (Jews who had adopted the Greek culture and language) did not think the widows in their group were getting their fair share, so they complained to the Hebraic (Hebrew-speaking) Jews (Acts 6:1). The twelve apostles appointed seven men to tend to the duty of food distribution (Acts 6:2–3). One of these men was Stephen. According to Acts 6:8, he was full of power and God's grace, and he performed great wonders and signs among the people. However, members of the synagogue began to argue with Stephen, but God gave him such great wisdom that they could not stand up against it (Acts 6:9–10).

Dave and I learned early in our ministry that if we wanted God's power, we had to keep strife out of the ministry and out of our home, and we work diligently to do so. If you intend to be a peacemaker, you will need to seek peace eagerly and make it a top priority in your life.

The Secret to Peace

Many people are unaware that there is a secret regarding having peace with other people. The secret is that before we can have peace with people, we must be at peace with God and at peace with ourselves. First Peter 3:10–11 (AMPC) says:

> *Before you can have peace with others, you must be at peace with God and with yourself.*

For let him who wants to enjoy life and see good days [good—whether apparent or not] keep his tongue free from evil and his lips from guile (treachery, deceit).

Let him turn away from wickedness and shun it, and let him do right. Let him search for peace (harmony; undisturbedness from fears, agitating passions, and moral conflicts) and seek it eagerly. [Do not merely desire peaceful relations with God, with your fellowmen, and with yourself, but pursue, go after them!]

Peace with God

Peace with God is maintained by having no hidden sin (sin for which we have not repented) in our life. God wants us to be truthful in our inmost being (Psalm 51:6). Of course, He already knows everything we have done, but we need to bring it out into the light and expose it. We need to talk with God about it, repent, and receive His forgiveness (1 John 1:9).

> You must walk in obedience to God's commands.

We also need to walk in obedience to God's commands, because if we don't, we will have a guilty conscience and forfeit our peace with God. The psalmist writes in Psalm 66:18: "If I regard iniquity in my heart, the Lord will not hear me" (AMPC). Hidden sin not only affects our peace, but it also hinders our prayers: "Whoever conceals their sins does not prosper, but the one who confesses and renounces them finds mercy" (Proverbs 28:13).

One of the first things I do each day is ask God to forgive any sins I have committed in word, thought, or deed. I do this because I want to begin each day at peace with God. If I do something wrong and am aware of it, I don't wait to repent. I do so right away, but I also begin my day with repentance and gratitude for all God is and all He does for us.

Peace with Ourselves

We can have peace with ourselves by receiving the forgiveness God freely offers us. We must also accept ourselves and not be continually finding something we don't like about ourselves. God created us carefully with His own hand in our mother's womb (Psalm 139:13), and we are not a mistake. Not liking yourself is equivalent to telling God He did a bad job when He created you. You are unique and not intended to be like someone else, so be diligent in resisting the temptation to compare yourself with other people.

We all do things we don't like, but we should love ourselves because God loves us. Loving ourselves is simply receiving God's love, which He freely gives to us. We have all sinned and come short of the glory of God (Romans 3:23), but we are also all justified freely by His grace (Romans 3:24). Receive His forgiveness, mercy, and justification and be at peace with yourself.

> Loving yourself is receiving God's love, which is freely given.

We will never be completely sin-free as long as we live in our flesh-and-bone bodies. We can and should improve and sin less and less as we grow closer to God, but we won't reach perfection until the Perfect One, Jesus, comes to take us home to heaven.

I was at war with myself for many years, and I couldn't love anyone else until I learned to love myself—not in a selfish, self-centered way, but in a balanced, godly way. If you don't have love inside of you, then you cannot give it away. I urge you to come to terms of peace with yourself. If I could give my younger self any advice, I would tell her to accept herself much earlier than she did. Only God can change us, and He does so little by little. No purpose is served by hating ourselves while God is changing us.

I wish I were gentler and more patient. I wish I were more creative and that I could read faster than I do. If I could change myself, I would adjust many things, but I can't, and thank God, I have finally stopped trying. I've learned to enjoy myself and realize that every human being has weaknesses and strengths. I focus on my strengths and pray about my weaknesses.

> Focus on your strengths and pray about your weaknesses.

Once you have peace with God and peace with yourself, you will be able to have peace with other people. You will still need to make an effort to do so, but it is worth it because God blesses the peacemakers.

8. Blessed Are Those Who Are Persecuted

Blessed and happy and enviably fortunate and spiritually prosperous (in the state in which the born-again child of God enjoys and finds satisfaction in God's favor and salvation, regardless of his outward conditions) are those who are persecuted for righteousness' sake (for being and doing right), for theirs is the kingdom of heaven! Blessed (happy, to be envied, and spiritually prosperous—with life-joy and satisfaction in God's favor and salvation, regardless of your outward conditions) are you when people revile you and persecute you and say all kinds of evil things against you falsely on My account. Be glad and supremely joyful, for your reward in heaven is great (strong and intense), for in this same way people persecuted the prophets who were before you.

Matthew 5:10–12 AMPC

Jesus' teaching in Matthew 5:10–12 is perhaps one of the most difficult to understand. How can we consider ourselves blessed when we are being persecuted for doing what is right? We share in Christ's sufferings when we do this because He was persecuted for doing what was right. His reward did come, and ours will also.

I went to church for many years and was a nominal Christian. I was not seriously committed and not fully surrendered to the Lord, but I had lots of friends. In 1976, God touched my life in a profound way, and it changed me forever. After that experience, I got serious about my relationship with Him and answered the call to ministry He placed on my life—to teach His Word. At that point, I lost friends and was gossiped about, judged, criticized, and even asked to leave my church. People I thought were good friends abandoned me, telling me I was wrong to pursue God's call. This was my first big test as a Christian who was on fire for God.

I was confused about the way people treated me because I felt I was following God. I had not yet learned that obeying Him does frequently entail some suffering, which can be the devil's way of attempting to stop us from advancing God's kingdom. The experience I am sharing was extremely difficult for me. I am grateful for God's grace, which helped me not to do what people wanted me to do to keep their friendship and enabled me to not give up.

Often, family members or other people will reject us if we fully surrender to God, because when we do, we may not be able to do everything we once did. We might have to say no to a movie they want to see, or no to a party where we know there will be drugs and heavy drinking of alcohol. Our interests will change, and we might prefer going to a Bible conference over going to Las Vegas for a weekend. The people close to us may feel convicted because of our choice to obey God, and to deflect how they feel, they find some fault in us.

If we remain lukewarm and not fully surrendered to God, the devil will leave us alone. But when we begin to get serious in our relation-

> *Worry if the devil is leaving you alone, not when he is attacking you.*

ship with God, he tries to stop us. I once heard that we should worry more if the devil is leaving us alone than we should if he is attacking us.

We Are Blessed When We Suffer

The idea that we are blessed when we suffer may seem strange. The apostle Peter writes that we should not be surprised when fiery ordeals come into our lives to test us (1 Peter 4:12). We never truly know how strong our faith is until some difficulty comes along to test it. Peter says we should rejoice when we face difficulties because we are participating in the sufferings of Christ, so that we "may be overjoyed when his glory is revealed" (1 Peter 4:13). If holding on to our faith seems hard at times now, we will be glad we did when Jesus returns to take us home.

Peter also writes that if we are insulted because of the name of Christ, we are blessed, "for the Spirit of glory and of God rests on you" (1 Peter 4:14). He goes on to say, "If you suffer, it should not be as a murderer or thief or any other kind of criminal, or even as a meddler. However, if you suffer as a Christian, do not be ashamed, but praise God that you bear that name" (1 Peter 4:15–16).

It is hard when suddenly no one wants to eat lunch with you at work or when you know people are gossiping about you. Under circumstances such as these, we can easily be tempted to try to defend ourselves. But God tells us to not even do that. Paul writes: "God is just: He will pay back trouble to those who trouble you and give relief to you who are troubled, and to us as well. This will happen when the Lord Jesus is revealed from heaven in blazing fire with his powerful angels" (2 Thessalonians 1:6–7). It is comforting to know that we can depend on God to deal with our enemies and to take care of us.

The apostle Peter also writes that a person "is regarded favorably (is approved, acceptable, and thankworthy) if, as in the sight of God, he endures the pain of unjust suffering" (1 Peter 2:19 AMPC). In other words, those who suffer for God are "regarded favorably." He goes on to say: "[After all] what kind of glory [is there in it] if, when you do wrong and are punished for it, you take it patiently? But if you bear patiently with suffering [which results] when you do right and that is undeserved, it is acceptable and pleasing to God" (1 Peter 2:20 AMPC).

The first time I heard these verses from 1 Peter 2, I didn't like them at all. But now I understand that it isn't the suffering that pleases God; it's bearing suffering patiently, with a good attitude, that pleases Him. Anyone can have a good attitude when everything is going their way, but God's grace is required to bear with suffering that is undeserved. Let me say it again: Your reward will come. Peter even goes so far as to say that if we have been called to suffer unjustly, we should remember that Christ suffered for us and left us to be His personal example (1 Peter 2:21 AMPC).

> Bearing suffering patiently is what pleases God, not the suffering itself.

The old Joyce didn't take anything off anybody or let anyone get away with doing anything she didn't like, so I have had to learn a lot regarding suffering and persecution. I have a strong sense of fairness, and if something is not fair, I want to come against it. Waiting on God is something I have had to learn, but it is the only way we will get our reward from Him.

Types of Persecution

People have differing ideas of what suffering means, perhaps because there are many types of suffering. They include:

- Physical suffering. In some countries, people are beaten, imprisoned, and even killed for being Christians. Peter, Paul, and many other early followers of Christ experienced this kind of persecution. There was a time in Rome when Christians were put into the arena and eaten by lions as a form of entertainment for the Romans.

- Rejection (being left out of things)
- Being made fun of, which causes embarrassment
- Being insulted
- Being judged critically (talked about and thought of in an unkind way)
- Being discriminated against (for example, being passed over for a promotion you have earned at work because you refuse to be dishonest)

God will reward you when you suffer. I now have favor with people who once rejected me. Let me close this chapter with this encouraging scripture: "The Lord works righteousness and justice for all the oppressed" (Psalm 103:6). When you are suffering, think about the reward that will come in the future, not the suffering of the present.

CHAPTER 21

The Doorway to Blessings

A contented mind is the greatest blessing a man can enjoy in this world.

Joseph Addison[46]

We often seek to be blessed without realizing that each and every moment we live is filled with blessings. We simply don't take time to see them. I'm breathing right now, and that is a blessing. I can see, and many people cannot. I can read and write, while more than 750 million people in the world are still illiterate. I have food in my refrigerator, while millions of people worldwide are on the brink of starvation. I could go on and on, but I think you would agree that we are already blessed, and perhaps one doorway to more blessings is being thankful for the ones we already have.

One thing is for sure, it is not our circumstances—good or bad—that determine our level of blessing; it is our perception of those circumstances. Someone with a positive attitude can have negative circumstances and be happier than someone with a negative attitude and positive circumstances. The opening quotation of this chapter says, "A contented mind is the greatest blessing a man can enjoy in this world." I agree. If our mind is content, we will be content with life through its ups and downs.

> *A positive attitude under negative circumstances is better than a negative attitude under positive circumstances.*

Compromising is what steals or blocks our blessings. *To compromise* means to do a little less than what we know to be right. The "little bit" of compromise often deceives us. We think a little bit can't possibly matter much, but it does.

> *Compromising is what blocks your blessings.*

Here's a practical example that demonstrates this principle: Let's say I made a batch of cookies. You have eaten cookies made by this recipe, and they are your favorite. But what if I told you that, this time, I put just a tiny, tiny bit of ant poison in them. Would you eat them? I know you wouldn't, and neither would I. But we do accept little bits of things that are bad for us or displeasing to God in other ways and think they don't matter.

If we do what is right, then we will be blessed. This is a guarantee in God's Word. He blesses obedience (Joshua 1:8; Isaiah 1:19; Luke 5:1–10).

Why Was Jesus Hated?

I think John 15:25 is one of the saddest scriptures in the Bible. Jesus said, "They hated me without reason." Why did they hate Him? I can think of several reasons:

- They hated Him because He was good, and they were not.
- They hated Him because His principles confronted theirs.
- They hated Him because He would not compromise.
- They hated Him because He refused to be mediocre.
- They hated Him because He was different from other people.

People hated Jesus for all these reasons and more, even though He was good. Doing right does not guarantee acceptance, approval, or applause, but God's Word says, "Let us not become weary in doing good, for at the proper time we will reap a harvest if we do not give up" (Galatians 6:9). I would rather have God's blessings than applause from humans anytime.

> *I would rather have God's blessings than human applause.*

Genesis 4:1–16 tells the story of two brothers, Cain and Abel. Cain was jealous of Abel's righteousness, and he killed him. He wanted what Abel had—God's approval—but he did not want to do what Abel was doing to get it.

According to Genesis 4:6, Cain was angry and downcast, as many compromisers are. They want to be blessed, but they don't choose to do what is right, and they live with the burden of a guilty conscience. They want the rewards of righteousness and the momentary fleshly pleasure of sin, which is not possible.

People sometimes pay a high price for a cheap thrill.

Abel brought God the firstborn of his flock as an offering, and Cain brought some of the fruit of the ground (Genesis 4:3–4). He kept some for himself, and I personally think he was greedy. He did not give all to God as Abel did. When Cain got angry, God asked him, "Why are you angry?...If you do what is right, will you not be accepted? But if you do not do what is right, sin is crouching at your door; it desires to have you, but you must rule over it" (Genesis 4:6–7). No one can do the wrong thing and get a right result.

Sometimes, to do the right thing we must choose the painful path, the one that includes some suffering. Hebrews 11:24–25 says this about Moses: "By faith Moses, when he had grown up, refused to be known as the son of Pharaoh's daughter. *He chose to be mistreated along with the people of God rather than to enjoy the fleeting pleasures of sin*" (emphasis mine).

> People sometimes pay a high price for a cheap thrill.

Moses was a special man. Not many people choose to suffer, as he did, when they could live in luxury. Numbers 12:3 says that when God called Moses to lead the Israelites out of Egypt into Canaan, he was said to be "a very humble man, more humble than anyone else on the face of the earth."

Humility or meekness is not weakness, as I mentioned earlier in the book; it is strength under control.

Waiting for the Reward

At times, we must keep doing what is right for a long time before we see any reward. This is why Galatians 6:9 says not to grow weary in doing good and that in due season we will reap if we don't give up. Don't do what is right to get a reward; do it because it is right and because you love God. And let God take care of rewards in His way and according to His timing.

The best antidote for greed is generosity.

Greed for gain is the reason for much compromise. The best antidote for greed is generosity. The more generous you are, the less likely you will be to become greedy. A Christian leader is not to be "a lover of money [insatiable for wealth and ready to obtain it by questionable means]" (1 Timothy 3:3 AMPC).

What Rewards Can We Expect?

God will give us many different types of rewards if we are obedient to Him, especially when we are being mistreated. We have already seen that He will give us a double blessing for former shame and mistreatment (Isaiah 61:7). Being obedient to God always involves forgiving the people who hurt you or treat you unjustly. It is vital that we let go of any unforgiveness in our hearts. I have mentioned this

Obedience to God means forgiving those who hurt you.

several times throughout this book, but it is an area that comes up in our lives over and over again: Staying free of unforgiveness, bitterness, and resentment requires vigilance and a determination to obey God.

When we are doing things God's way, we can expect a reward when the time is right. But what are those rewards? Some of them are unique to the individual, but many are the same for all of us, including:

- *God Himself.* The blessing of having God in our lives is the biggest reward of all. Serving Him is a privilege, not an obligation. David said that God was his portion (Psalm 16:5). And Hebrews 11:6 says God is the rewarder of those who earnestly seek Him. The more obedient we are to God, the closer we will be to Him.
- *God's favor.* Psalm 5:12 says: "Surely, Lord, you bless the righteous; you surround them with your favor as with a shield."
- *The crown of life.* According to James 1:12, "Blessed is the one who perseveres under trial because, having stood the test, that person will receive the crown of life that the Lord has promised to those who love him."
- *Authority.* According to Proverbs 12:24, "Diligent hands will rule, but laziness ends in forced labor." People who are diligent will keep doing God's will no matter how they feel.
- *The rewards of generosity.* Deuteronomy 15:10 says: "Give generously to them and do so without a grudging heart; then because of this the Lord your God will bless you in all your work and in everything you put your hand to." And Matthew 6:3–4 says: "When you give to the needy, do not let your left hand know what your right hand is doing, so that your giving may be in secret. Then your Father, who sees what is done in secret, will reward you."
- *Answered prayer.* First John 3:21–22 says: "Dear friends, if our hearts do not condemn us, we have confidence before God

and receive from him anything we ask, because we keep his commands and do what pleases him" (emphasis mine).

- *Peace.* According to Psalm 119:165, "great peace" is given to those who love God's law, and "nothing can make them stumble."
- *Heaven.* Heaven is our final reward. What a wonderful place it is—no death, no tears, no pain (Revelation 21:4). We will see God face-to-face, and everything will be made new (Revelation 21:3, 5). We will see beauty beyond anything we could even imagine, and I'm sure the atmosphere is one of total peace, joy, and love. I personally can't wait to get there, but I am also content to be here serving God until He is ready to take me home.

No matter what happens in a person's life and no matter how negative or painful it may be, God can make it work out for the good of those who love Him and want His will (Romans 8:28). I know this from God's Word, from my own experience, and from the testimony of thousands of other people: *No matter how big of a mess you have in your life, or how big of a mess you are yourself, if you follow the guidance of the Holy Spirit and desire to be obedient to God, He will bring a double blessing into your life.* Don't think it is too late for you, because it is never too late to begin.

Let me clarify that all of God's goodness is by His grace. We don't earn it by our works; we access the blessings of God by faith. And it is impossible to have true faith without desiring to be obedient to God and growing steadily in it.

If you have never done so, I urge you to make a full surrender to God. Turn everything over to Him and get ready to be excited as you watch Him work all things out for your good.

All of us go through times in our lives when we say, "This situation is a mess!" We may be talking about a challenge in a relationship, a family conflict, a financial problem, a situation at work, a moral dilemma, difficulties in some group or organization we are involved with, the state of the world, or conditions in our home. We may even be talking about ourselves. A mess is a problem, a difficult situation, or a complicated set of circumstances—and it can happen anywhere, anytime, to anyone. Jesus tells us that in the world we will have tribulation (John 16:33). He also says in the same verse that we should cheer up because He has overcome the world.

I wish I could tell you that after reading this book, you won't encounter any more messes in your life. But that's simply not true. What I do hope is that after reading it, you will be better equipped than ever to deal with the messes that are inevitable in life. I hope you'll be

> *In Jesus, you have everything you need.*

reminded of the lessons you've learned through these pages, and that they will give you exactly the advice, encouragement, and biblical truth you need to experience blessing in the midst of a mess. Paul writes that right in the middle of trouble and difficulties we are more than conquerors through Christ, who loves us (Romans 8:36–37). According to 2 Corinthians 2:14 (AMPC), Jesus always leads us in triumph, and in Him, you have everything you need to be victorious over any mess life brings your way.

In addition, I hope you'll remember that Jesus gave us keys to blessing when He taught the Beatitudes in His Sermon on the Mount. Each attitude or character quality He mentions has a blessing attached to it, and as you develop these qualities in your life, you will experience greater blessings.

I know life isn't always easy and smooth, and I pray that no matter what messy situation you may go through, you will be increasingly blessed in the midst of it. I also pray that you will experience a double reward for any trouble you go through. Remain steadfast no matter what your circumstances may be. Continue serving and thanking God, and the blessings you receive will far outweigh the difficulty you dealt with.

1. *Words of Art: Inspiring Quotes from the Masters* (Adams Media, 2012).

2. G. V. Wigram, *Gleanings from the Teaching of G. V. Wigram* (Bible Truth Publishers, n.d.), 274.

3. Quoted at ChristianQuotes.info, https://www.christianquotes.info /quotes-by-author/augustine-quotes.

4. Abraham Lincoln, letter to Edward Stanton, July 14, 1864.

5. Matshona Dhliwayo, quoted at https://www.goodreads.com/quotes /9542059.

6. Edmund Clowney, *The Message of 1 Peter* (InterVarsity Press, 2021), 34–35.

7. James Strong, *Strong's Concordance of the Bible*, https://biblehub.com /hebrew/835.htm.

8. Quoted at SermonQuotes.com, https://sermonquotes.com/max-lu cado-2/11165-god-loves-us-much-indulge-every-whim-max-lucado .html.

9. Brant Hansen, *Unoffendable: How Just One Change Can Make All of Life Better* (Thomas Nelson, 2015), 184.

10. Quoted at Ziglar.com, https://www.ziglar.com/quotes/your-attitude -not-your-aptitude.

11. Quoted at Quote Fancy, https://quotefancy.com/quote/841058/John -C-Maxwell-You-are-only-an-attitude-away-from-success.

12. Quoted at Healing for Eating Disorders, https://healingforeating disorders.com/recovery-quotes-for-eating-disorders-2.

13. Quoted at Quote Fancy, https://quotefancy.com/quote/841585/John -C-Maxwell-Circumstances-do-not-make-you-what-you-are-they -reveal-what-you-are.

14. Quoted at Quote Master, https://www.quotemaster.org/q8b205 70004ab0d75c969e63badcefa09.

15. Quoted in Stephanie A. Sarkis, "50 Quotes on Perspective," *Psychology Today*, October 25, 2012, https://www.psychologytoday.com/us /blog/here-there-and-everywhere/201210/50-quotes-perspective.

16. "Acid Attack Survivor Katie Piper Is Moving On and Helping Others," God Vine, January 22, 2023, https://www.godvine.com/read/acid-attack-survivor-katie-piper-1484.html.

17. Quoted at A to Z Quotes, https://www.azquotes.com/quote/540419.

18. A. W. Tozer, *Of God and Men* (Christian Publications, 1960).

19. Google English Dictionary provided by Oxford Languages.

20. "Stress," Cleveland Clinic, https://my.clevelandclinic.org/health/articles/11874-stress.

21. "Stress Symptoms: Effects on Your Body and Behavior," Mayo Clinic, https://www.mayoclinic.org/healthy-lifestyle/stress-management/in-depth/stress-symptoms/art-20050987.

22. Carol Krueger, *The Spider and the King* (Rigby, 1999).

23. Quoted at Brainy Quote, https://www.brainyquote.com/quotes/meister_eckhart_149158.

24. Quoted at Quote Fancy, https://quotefancy.com/quote/899530/Rick-Warren-If-you-give-it-to-God-He-transforms-your-test-into-a-testimony-your-mess-into.

25. A. W. Tozer, *The Knowledge of the Holy* (Harper and Row, 1961).

26. Jonathan Edwards, *The Works of President Edwards*, vol. 7 (G. & C. & H. Carvill, 1830), 410.

27. Philip Yancey, *Reaching for the Invisible God: What Can We Expect to Find?* (Zondervan, 2002), 95.

28. C. S. Lewis, *The Problem of Pain* (HarperOne, 2015), 91, 93–94.

29. Quoted at Christian Quotes, https://www.christianquotes.info/quotes-by-author/andrew-murray-quotes.

30. Quoted at Quote Fancy, https://quotefancy.com/quote/1552435/Teresa-of-vila-You-pay-God-a-compliment-by-asking-great-things-of-Him.

31. "Strong's #6793," Old Testament Hebrew Lexical Dictionary, https://www.studylight.org/lexicons/eng/hebrew/6743.html.

32. "Strong's #2137," Old Testament Hebrew Lexical Dictionary, https://www.studylight.org/lexicons/eng/hebrew/2137.html.

33. Quoted at Wise Famous Quotes, https://www.wisefamousquotes.com/henri-j-m-nouwen-quotes/becoming-a-child-is-living-the-beatitudes-and-82167.

34. "Beatitude," *Cambridge Advanced Learner's Dictionary and Thesaurus*, https://dictionary.cambridge.org/us/dictionary/english/beatitude.

35. Noah Webster, "Virtue," *An American Dictionary of the English Language* (S. Converse, 1828), https://webstersdictionary1828.com/Dictionary/virtue.

36. Quoted at Brainy Quote, https://www.brainyquote.com/quotes/rick_warren_395865.

37. Quoted at Brainy Quote, https://www.brainyquote.com/quotes/henry_ward_beecher_105506.

38. Quoted at Oxford Reference, https://www.oxfordreference.com/display/10.1093/acref/9780191843730.001.0001/q-oro-ed5-00006699.

39. *New Spirit-Filled Life Bible* (Thomas Nelson, 2002), xxiv.

40. Matthew Henry, *Commentary on the Whole Bible*, vol. 5 (Fleming Revell, n.d.), 51.

41. Henry, 51.

42. "Katharos," Bible Study Tools, https://www.biblestudytools.com/lexicons/greek/nas/katharos.html.

43. *New Spirit-Filled Life Bible*, 1821.

44. "What Does It Mean to Be Pure in Heart?" Got Questions, https://www.gotquestions.org/pure-in-heart.html.

45. Eleanor Roosevelt, *Voice of America* broadcast, November 11, 1951.

46. Joseph Addison, "No. 574" (July 30, 1714), *The Spectator* (H. Washbourne and Co., 1857), 656.

Do you have a real relationship with Jesus?

God loves you! He created you to be a special, unique, one-of-a-kind individual, and He has a specific purpose and plan for your life. And through a personal relationship with your Creator—God—you can discover a way of life that will truly satisfy your soul.

No matter who you are, what you've done, or where you are in your life right now, God's love and grace are greater than your sin—your mistakes. Jesus willingly gave His life so you can receive forgiveness from God and have new life in Him. He's just waiting for you to invite Him to be your Savior and Lord.

If you are ready to commit your life to Jesus and follow Him, all you have to do is ask Him to forgive your sins and give you a fresh start in the life you are meant to live. Begin by praying this prayer...

> *Lord Jesus, thank You for giving Your life for me and forgiving me of my sins so I can have a personal relationship with You. I am sincerely sorry for the mistakes I've made, and I know I need You to help me live right.*
>
> *Your Word says in Romans 10:9, "If you declare with your mouth, 'Jesus is Lord,' and believe in your heart that God raised him from the dead, you will be saved" (NIV). I believe You are the Son of God and confess You as my Savior and Lord. Take me just as I am, and work in my heart, making me the person You want me to be. I want to live for You, Jesus, and I am so grateful that You are giving me a fresh start in my new life with You today.*
>
> *I love You, Jesus!*

It's so amazing to know that God loves us so much! He wants to have a deep, intimate relationship with us that grows every day as we spend time with Him in prayer and Bible study. And we want to encourage you in your new life in Christ.

Please visit joycemeyer.org/KnowJesus to request Joyce's book *A New Way of Living*, which is our gift to you. We also have other free resources online to help you make progress in pursuing everything God has for you.

Congratulations on your fresh start in your life in Christ! We hope to hear from you soon.

Joyce Meyer is one of the world's leading practical Bible teachers and a *New York Times* bestselling author. Joyce's books have helped millions of people find hope and restoration through Jesus Christ. Joyce's program, *Enjoying Everyday Life*, is broadcast on television and radio and online to millions worldwide in over one hundred languages.

Through Joyce Meyer Ministries, Joyce teaches internationally on a number of topics with a particular focus on how the Word of God applies to our everyday lives. Her candid communication style allows her to share openly and practically about her experiences so others can apply what she has learned to their lives.

Joyce has authored more than 140 books, which have been translated into more than 160 languages, and over 39 million of her books have been distributed worldwide. Bestsellers include *Power Thoughts*; *The Confident Woman*; *Look Great, Feel Great*; *Starting Your Day Right*; *Ending Your Day Right*; *Approval Addiction*; *How to Hear from God*; *Beauty for Ashes*; and *Battlefield of the Mind*.

Joyce's passion to help people who are hurting is foundational to the vision of Hand of Hope, the missions arm of Joyce Meyer Ministries. Each year Hand of Hope provides millions of meals for the hungry and malnourished, installs freshwater wells in poor and remote areas, provides critical relief after natural disasters, and offers free medical and dental care to thousands through their hospitals and clinics worldwide. Through Project GRL, women and children are rescued from human trafficking and provided safe places to receive an education, nutritious meals, and the love of God.

Joyce Meyer Ministries—South Africa
P.O. Box 5
Cape Town 8000
South Africa
(27) 21-701-1056

Joyce Meyer Ministries—Francophonie
29 avenue Maurice Chevalier
77330 Ozoir la Ferriere
France

Joyce Meyer Ministries—Germany
Postfach 761001
22060 Hamburg
Germany
+49 (0)40 / 88 88 4 11 11

Joyce Meyer Ministries—Netherlands
Lorenzlaan 14
7002 HB Doetinchem
+31 657 555 9789

Joyce Meyer Ministries—Russia
P.O. Box 789
Moscow 101000
Russia
+7 (495) 727-14-68

100 Inspirational Quotes
100 Ways to Simplify Your Life
21 Ways to Finding Peace and Happiness
The Answer to Anxiety
Any Minute
Approval Addiction
The Approval Fix
Authentically, Uniquely You*
The Battle Belongs to the Lord
Battlefield of the Mind*
Battlefield of the Mind Bible
Battlefield of the Mind for Kids
Battlefield of the Mind for Teens
Battlefield of the Mind Devotional
Battlefield of the Mind New Testament
Be Anxious for Nothing*
Being the Person God Made You to Be
Beauty for Ashes
Change Your Words, Change Your Life
Colossians: A Biblical Study
The Confident Mom
The Confident Woman
The Confident Woman Devotional
Do It Afraid*
Do Yourself a Favor . . . Forgive
Eat the Cookie . . . Buy the Shoes
Eight Ways to Keep the Devil under Your Feet
Ending Your Day Right
Enjoying Where You Are on the Way to Where You Are Going
Ephesians: A Biblical Study
The Everyday Life Bible
The Everyday Life Psalms and Proverbs
Filled with the Spirit
Galatians: A Biblical Study
Good Health, Good Life
Habits of a Godly Woman
Healing the Soul of a Woman*
Healing the Soul of a Woman Devotional
Hearing from God Each Morning
How to Age without Getting Old
How to Hear from God*
How to Succeed at Being Yourself
How to Talk with God

Trusting God Day by Day
The Word, the Name, the Blood
Woman to Woman
You Can Begin Again
Your Battles Belong to the Lord*

BOOKS BY DAVE MEYER

Life Lines